Library and Learning Resource Programs:
Evaluation and Self-Study

CJCLS Guide #3

Edited by

Wanda K. Johnston

Community and Junior College Library Section
Association of College and Research Libraries
A division of the American Library Association
Chicago 1998

The paper used in this publication meets the minimum requirements of American National Standard for Information Sciences–Permanence of Paper for Printed Library Materials, ANSI Z39.48-1992. ∞

Library of Congress Cataloging-in-Publication Data
Library and learning resource prgrams : evaluation and self-study /
 edited by Wanda K. Johnston.
        p.   cm. -- (CJCLS guide ; #3)
   Includes bibliographical references (p.   ) and index.
   ISBN 0-8389-7989-0 (alk. paper)
    1. Community college libraries--United States--Evaluation.
  2. Junior college libraries--United States--Evaluation.
  I. Johnston, Wanda K. II. Association of College and Research
  Libraries. Community and Junior College Libraries Section.
  III. Series.
  Z675.J8L49 1998
  027.7'0973--dc21   98-33959

Printed in the United States of America.

02 01 00 99 98   5 4 3 2 1

CONTENTS

INTRODUCTION

The July 1, 1998, Federal Register announced regulations focusing on educational effectiveness which accrediting agencies must follow. (see appendix) These regulations include requiring colleges to have mission statements, to document the educational achievements of their students, to admit students who can benefit from instruction, and to systematically take steps to enhance student achievement. Thus, for colleges to receive accreditation, they must participate in assessment and planning cycles by developing mission statements, establishing goals and objectives, following action plans, and assessing educational effectiveness. As a unit of the college, the library/learning resources department also participates in this college-wide assessment and planning process. Ultimately, this program assessment not only demonstrates institutional effectiveness but also improves performance.

These regulations require accrediting agencies to systematically obtain and consider substantial and accurate information on the educational effectiveness of postsecondary institutions or programs. The Council on Postsecondary Accreditation (COPA) defines postsecondary accreditation as:

> "a process by which an institution or a specialized unit of postsecondary education periodically evaluates its educational activities and seeks an independent judgment by peers that it achieves substantially its own educational objectives and meets the established standards of a body from which it seeks accreditation. Generally, the accreditation process involves (1) a clear statement of the institution's or unit's objectives, (2) a self-study by the institution or unit which examines its activities in relation to those objectives, (3) an on-site evaluation by a selected group of peers which reports to the accrediting body, and (4) a decision by this independent body that the institution or unit does or does not meet its standards for accreditation." (Sacks 5)

Accrediting associations include regional, specialized, and state agencies. The six regional associations review the college as a whole and focus on its mission and goals as central to the institution's existence and purpose. Each regional accreditation association establishes its own criteria and procedures within the COPA definition. Each member college is formally visited only every five to ten years unless it is experiencing difficulties or undergoing rapid change. The college's annual or periodic reports demonstrate its self-regulation toward compliance. In addition to supporting the general institutional effectiveness requirements, library/learning resources departments must comply with specific criteria which varies from association to association; however, the department's continued annual or periodic program review assessment and reporting also demonstrates voluntary self-regulation. (see appendix)

More than fifty specialized accrediting agencies recognized by COPA oversee self-regulatory function for specific programs. Their standards commonly include statements on the organization and governance of the program, faculty qualification and teaching loads, admission and retention of students, curriculum and course descriptions, library resources, facilities and equipment, and financial support. As with the regional accrediting agencies, the specific criteria for library/learning resources programs vary from agency to agency.

State agencies vary greatly with their statutory powers, organizational structures, scope of authority, and approached to evaluation. Generally, they are involved with new program approval, programs requiring licensing and certification, and shared comprehensive program review.

In Preparing for Accreditation, Sacks and Whildin note that all regional associations and many of the specialized accrediting agencies have criteria regarding the academic library/learning resources program. Frequently cited topics include:
- The library's importance as an academic resource.
- The importance of mission, goals, and objectives in supporting the purposes of the library's constituencies.
- The relationship of the library's resources and services to its parent institution's instructional and research goals and programs.
- The quality (nature, scope, and size) of collections, staff, and physical facilities.
- The availability of access services enabling the user to locate and use information not locally available.
- Reference, library instruction, and referral assistance to enable the user to identify, select, and use information resources.
- The nature and extent of collections and services.
- The financial and organizational abilities to support the faculty and student needs.
- The mechanisms used to communicate with constituents. (Sacks 11-12)

In compliance with federal regulations, accrediting associations encourage ongoing evaluation of the library/learning resources program's effectiveness through program review activities which describe the program, assess its strengths and weaknesses, and plan toward the future. Through this systematic and regular assessment and planning, the library/learning resources program maintains and continually improves its educational effectiveness within the college as a whole.

Works Cited

Blandy, Susan Griswold. "The Librarians Role in Academic Assessment and
    Accreditation: A Case Study." Assessment and Accountability in Reference
    Work. Ed Susan Blandy et al. New York: Haworth Press, 1992. 69-87.
Sacks, Patricia Ann and Sara Lou Whildin. Preparing for Accreditation: A Handbook for
    Librarians. Chicago: American Library Association, 1993.

SURVEY REVIEW

The inception of this project occurred when the editor returned from a regional accreditation visitation during which the team had lengthy discussions of what constituted institutional effectiveness and specific program success. The editor noted that library/learning resources personnel regularly evaluate their programs to determine if they are successful and to plan for the future. Minimally, they gather statistics for the Integrated Postsecondary Education Data System (IPEDS), for their College's annual planning and budgeting process, and for regional and specialized accreditation visits. Thus, based upon the editor's experience and the cooperative nature of library/learning resources personnel, she felt that a "sampler" of how such quantitative and qualitative information are gathered, compiled, and reported might be useful for colleagues seeking to develop the most effective library/learning resources program and to integrate that program into the overall institutional effectiveness plan.

HISTORY

This manual is the third in the CJCLS Guide Series, following the popular Collection Management in the Electronic Age and A Copyright Sampler. The Guide Series grew out of the CJCLS Research and Publications Committee, chaired by Beverley Gass of Guilford Technical Community College (NC). The committee's goal was to encourage and sponsor ACRL publications relating directly to two-year academic institutions. The series was modeled after the ACRL CLIP Notes. Funding for the project was granted through the ACRL New Publications Committee.

In February 1998, the "CJCLS Library/Learning Resources Program Review Survey" (see appendix) was mailed to 807 members of the Community and Junior College Libraries Section. After the April 1 response deadline, a reminder was posted on the CJC-L listserv inviting anyone who had not responded to please do so and anyone wishing to participate who had not been contacted to respond. By June 1, eighty-five librarians, or 12% of those surveyed, returned useable completed surveys.

Initially, the editor was concerned by the low rate of return until one Director questioned the semantics of "program review." Another, noted that she would share information but preferred to keep specific statistical data confidential. Yet another willingly would share electronic statistical reports individually but was concerned about who held the report format copyrights, the library automation vendor or the user. This guide was created through contributions from twenty-four community college library/learning resources departments and with the assistance of Jo Ann Alexander, Learning Resources Department Staff Assistant at Central Florida Community College.

SURVEY SUMMARIES

Survey respondents represent a range of institution sizes. Approximately half of the library/learning resources departments are in institutions with fewer that 3000 full-time equivalent students and have fewer than ten full-time staff. Fifty-six (66%) of the respondents indicated that they participated in regional accreditation reviews, 51 (60%) in department self-assessment and planning, 39 (46%) in institutional strategic planning, 31 (36%) in annual reports, 19 (22%) in state program reviews, and 5 (6%) in specialized accreditation reviews. As might be expected, the library/learning resources director (84%) and library/learning resources staff (78%) most often conduct the program review assisted by college faculty (54%), the regional accreditation self study committee (51%), college students (46%), college administration (42%), and Library/Learning Resources Advisory Committee (28%).

Both quantitative and qualitative data are included in the program review process. Annual statistical data (86%), user satisfaction surveys/output measures (67%), and goal accomplishment (58%) are cited as the most used measures followed by comparative statistics using the ACRL/AECT Standards (41%), longitudinal statistics (35%), and comparative statistics from other colleges (33%).

Circulation of resources (89%), usually tracked through an online system, are the most frequently cited statistical data compiled. More than half of the respondents also count library instruction classes (80%), interlibrary loan (76%), on site collection size (75%), reference transactions (65%), and facilities use (65%). Other data compiled includes faculty audiovisual equipment use (48%), teleconferences (21%), media production services (20%), and audiovisual equipment repairs (8%).

User satisfaction surveys/output measures are used by 67% of the respondents. These measure general program satisfaction (62%), general program use (54%), library instruction (42%), collection holdings and access (40%), and reference service (38%). Lesser mentioned measures include informal suggestion box input (29%), audiovisual equipment service (25%), interlibrary loan success (24%), and media production (12%).

A full compilation of survey results is included in the Appendix.

REPORTS AND PLANS

Library/learning resources reviews gather both quantitative and qualitative data providing a "reality check" of current program effectiveness and plan toward increased future program effectiveness. Creation of these review reports result from adherence to regional and specialized accreditation requirements, campus-wide institutional effectiveness and strategic planning cycles, or internal departmental reviews. In "External Library Reviews: Issues and Approaches," Sarah M. Pritchard suggests:

"The basic effectiveness of the library should be studied, including
- the patterns and adequacy of its activities (administration, planning, public services, and technical services) and
- its resources (budget, staff, space, collections, technology, and systems).

In looking at the outcome of these, reviewers can try to assess:
- general levels of user satisfaction,
- professional development of services and staff,
- adherence to standards, and
- the centrality of the library in the educational endeavor of the campus." (4)

Pasadena City College, Canada College, and City College of San Francisco provide examples of annual reviews which incorporate the breadth of review suggested by Pritchard. Due to it's length, only the table of contents from the City College of San Francisco Program Review is included. Elaine P. Nunez Community College and Edmonds Community College complete their annual reviews following prescribed college-wide reporting formats.

Central Florida Community College follows a cyclical long-range planning process to ensure continued institutional effectiveness. It begins with establishing a mission, setting goals, developing plans, implementing plans, evaluating progress, and revising goals and plans in a renewal of the cycle. Within this process, the learning resources department is asked to create tactical plans, or short-term projects, which help achieve the college's strategic goals. Austin Community College and Macomb Community College follow similar institutional effectiveness cycles.

More complex planning documents are shared through Austin Community College's "Transition to the Future: LRS Strategic Plan 1998-2002" and Pasadena City College's "Shatford Library: Library Technology Master Plan 1997-2001." Additional annual report formats may be gleaned from Annual Reports for College Libraries: CLIP Note #10 and other resources cited in the bibliography.

External reviews usually are convened in adherence to regional, state, and other specialized accreditation processes. Most prevalent are regional accreditations. The library/learning resources criteria in the six regional accreditation associations, included in the appendix, are general in nature and differ among associations. Thus, as long as the library/learning resources department maintains effective internal program review and planning and adheres to the specific criteria of its regional accreditation association, it should remain in compliance. Since the "Standards for Community, Junior, and Technical College Learning Resources Programs" tend to be more precise, they frequently are integrated into the accreditation self-study.

Five of the regional accreditation agencies always, or almost always, include a librarian as a member of every peer evaluation team. The application process varies greatly, but most frequently the regional accrediting agency receives recommendations from librarians or institutional administrators. Application procedures may be found in "Are You Qualified to Serve on the Accreditation Team?" by William N. Nelson or by contacting your regional agency directly. Addresses are appended.

An example of a comprehensive statewide program review is the Level III Program Review of the state's community college library/learning resources centers commissioned by the Florida State Board of Community Colleges. The goal of the study was to determine the role library/learning resources programs should play in the community colleges, to identify current strengths and weaknesses, and offer recommendations which would ultimately improve the lives of students in the Florida community colleges.

The South Carolina Commission on Higher Education address libraries in their internal assessment of institutional effectiveness. Librarians gather statistics and data, survey patrons, evaluate reports, and analyze trends, all of which assess library resources and services on a regular basis and help libraries respond to student needs. Spartanburg Technical College is cited for its exemplary efforts in library assessment with an instructional emphasis. Specifically, the college library compiles a curricular program review packet which includes program related periodicals list, periodical spreadsheet, three-year acquisitions report, and library instruction report demonstrating that all one year curricula have at least six library assignments and associate degree programs have at least twelve. In addition, program faculty are asked to address whether library resources are adequate to meet program needs.

STATISTICAL REPORTS

Every community college library/learning resources program must complete the IPEDS federal data collection process every two years. This survey compiles data about library staff, operating expenses, library collections and services, and electronic services. The IPEDS survey indicates that congress uses the data to assess the need for revisions of existing legislation concerning libraries and the allocation of federal funds. Federal agencies need the data to evaluate and administer library programs. State education agencies and college librarians and administrators use the data for regional and national comparisons of library resources to plan for the effective use of funds. Finally, library associations and researchers use the survey results to determine the status of library operations and the profession. Further information may be obtained by calling a Bureau of Census IPEDS representative at (800) 451-6236.

Compilation of statistical data for the IPEDS survey or other reporting utilizes a combination of automated and manual methods. With library automation comes the capability for increased computer generated reports. For example, the Florida College Center for Library Automation boasts the provision of nearly two hundred statistical reports. Tarrant County Junior College has added a free statistical "counter" (http://www.showstat.com) on their homepage and Internet gateway page to count on and off-campus use. The manual "chit mark" system still is popular for reference statistics and the calendar system for library instruction counts. To simplify the statistic gathering process, many libraries use the sample week estimation process. In this process, a sample week, preferably the first full week of October, is chosen and record made of all activity counted. This activity is then entered into the formula: Sample Week Figure x 4 = Sample October Total. Then the Sample October Total is generalized into a sample year estimate.

Austin Community College and Central Florida Community College share their annual longitudinal statistic reports while Central Florida Community College, West Valley College, and Bunker Hill Community College share their monthly report formats.

Measuring Academic Library Performance: A Practical Approach, Assessment System for the Evaluation of Learning Resources Programs in Community Colleges, and Output Measures Manual for Community College Learning Resource Programs and Libraries, listed in the bibliography, provide additional practical statistic gathering and reporting suggestions.

USER SATISFACTION

User satisfaction surveys and suggestion box input most commonly augment informal feedback to determine general user satisfaction. Most prevalent are general user satisfaction surveys. Eight colleges shared their survey forms which were distributed to all library users when they visited the library. Generally, these surveys ask basic demographic information, the frequency of library visits, the purposes of these visits, and rate the success/satisfaction with the visits.

Three colleges adapted their user satisfaction form for student responses. Central Florida Community College also sought responses from students who did not use LRC services in addition to those who did. Consequently, they identified faculty members teaching freshman and sophomore level classes in all academic divisions. These faculty members distributed the survey during class, explained the purpose, and asked students to return the completed survey during the next class period. In addition, blank surveys were available at both Circulation and Reference Desks.

Four colleges shared their faculty user satisfaction surveys. Most colleges mail faculty surveys to all faculty or distribute them at division meetings. Corning Community College incorporates faculty survey into the curricular program review process, e.g. Nursing. Library staff complete a curricula related self-study focusing on the program under review. This self-study is distributed during a department meeting at which faculty are asked to discuss specific recommendations for the improvement or development of Library/Media resources relevant to the program and to suggest new resources or initiatives with information resources, services, technology, and new innovations.

Central Florida Community College shares its "Reference Satisfaction Survey" while Technical College of the Lowcountry and Nunez Community College share their library instruction surveys. Broome Community College provides a sample suggestion box form. The bibliography suggests additional general and specific user satisfaction survey forms.

PROGRAM REVIEW AND THE PLANNING CYCLE

Whether through an annual report, institutional effectiveness form, budget justification, or accreditation self-study, library/learning resources program review results are compiled routinely in nearly every community college as part of a long range planning cycle. The first stage of this cycle, the evaluation/needs assessment stage, asks the question "Where is the program now?" in terms of collections, services, personnel, and facilities. Statistical data, user input, past goal accomplishment, accreditation criteria, and national standards and trends are analyzed within the overall college mission and college-wide effectiveness plan.

The next stage, the long-range strategic planning stage, asks "Where do we want the program to be in the future?" Library/learning resources staff, advisory committee members, and others review the department mission and goals and the assessment conclusions to identify service needs, pet projects, and program potentials. These ideas are then evaluated within the framework of the college mission, goals, and parameters. Acceptable department objectives are ranked by chronological priority and feasibility within the constraints of anticipated human and fiscal resources in a one- to five-year span creating the long-range plan.

Finally, a short-range action plan is developed addressing implementation by asking "How will we get the program where we want it?" Objectives assigned for the year are charted noting objective, corresponding activities, timeline, and evaluation. Then implementation begins.

By documenting this evaluation/assessment, long-range planning, and action plan in the annual report or effectiveness plan, library/learning resources staff demonstrates its accountability for effectively meeting the college's library/learning resources needs. By following this planning cycle and publicizing its results, the Library/Learning Resources Director further increases program accountability, encourages further program development, and demonstrates educational effectiveness.

Works Cited

Nelson, William N. "Are You Qualified to Serve on the Accreditation Team?" C&RL News 59 (April 1998): 269-272.

Pritchard, Sarah M. "External Library Reviews: Issues and Approaches." Library Issues: Briefings for Faculty and Administrators 15 (November 1994): 1-6.

REPORTS AND PLANS

Annual Reviews
Pasadena City College
Canada College
City College of San Francisco
Elaine P. Nunez Community College
Edmonds Community College

Institutional Effectiveness Reports
Central Florida Community College
Austin Community College
Macomb Community College

Strategic Plan
Austin Community College

Technology Plan
Pasadena City College

Statewide Review
Florida State Board of Community Colleges

Shatford Library
Services, Staffing, Collections
1993-1996

A Report to the Board of Trustees
Pasadena City College

Submitted by

Mary Ann Laun
June 1996

Introduction

As educational institutions face the challenges of today's diverse societies and diverse information needs, connections become viable tools to manage the resources that meet those challenges. Student connections, college connections, and connections that extend beyond the college's physical boundaries are the springboards for meeting the college's educational mission and goals.

The library seeks to connect high quality information services and resources to the college community, whether it is in support of faculty in instructional activities, in provision of student learning opportunities to supplement and augment the curriculum, or in the creation of lifelong learning experiences. The Shatford Library encourages an environment where freedom of inquiry, thought, and expression are fostered. This environment is accessible to the library's diverse clientele with a sensitivity and acceptance of the multicultural backgrounds and needs of individual students. In addition, access is not limited with regard to origin, age, gender, sexual orientation, background, views or physical abilities.

◆ *Services*

A service philosophy within this college's environment cultivates personal accountability, respect for diversity, and responsiveness to the needs of all facets of the campus community. Sensitivity to issues of access and a variety of learning differences and backgrounds enhance the services the library provides. For example, as new technologies are developed and integrated into traditional services, it is imperative that these technologies enable users to connect resources to their individual goals and lifelong learning. The library staff seeks to meet these objectives by integrating library services in the following ways:

- One on one instruction to students at service desks, and to faculty and staff as needed
- Group instruction custom designed to meet discipline-specific needs
- Cultivation and maintenance of a dynamic collection of books, pamphlets, periodicals, newspapers, media, and electronic sources of information
- Preparation of bibliographies for use by instructors, staff and students
- Extension of the collection through the Internet, databases, and interlibrary loan services
- Liaison with faculty and staff to identify specific student needs for services and collections
- Service on campus committees, particularly related to curriculum, instruction, technology, and professional issues

Notable service accomplishments: 1993-1996
- Use of the library has *risen over 61%*; circulation of library materials has increased *47%*
- Students receiving library orientations increased *72%*
- Conducted an extensive student user survey (1200 respondents)
- Took the lead for faculty, staff, and student instruction on the use and resources of the Internet
- Participated in the development of the Technology Master Plan and campus Web page
- Delivered electronic, full-text periodicals service
- Received an ASB grant to fund 5 multimedia, Internet accessible workstations with laser printer (1996)
- Incorporated a Kurzweil Reading Edge system for students with disabilities (part of the DPSS project grant)
- Designed and installed software for a multimedia, graphical interface to Shatford Library services and collections
- Awarded the John Cotton Dana Special Award for Excellence in Public Relations (1995)
- Granted an ASB continuing grant to fund the textbook collection (1993-1995)
- Received the Silver Medallion for Shatford library brochure (1993)

Concerns for Special Needs

The 1995 User Survey (Appendix 1) cited significant factors for the library's service considerations:

- 67% of the students surveyed in 1995 said that they use the library daily, weekly, or monthly
- 56% of students *generally* find information that they need; 36% of students *partially* find information that they need
- 23% of students found that information was *too old*; 35% found *too little*
- 80% found that the information they found was an appropriate *level* for their needs
- 29% of students felt that the library was not open long enough to meet their needs
- 72% felt comfortable using computers in the library
- 17% excellent overall rating; 59% good; 22% fair; 2% poor

Self-Study Plans, 1995/1996-

These plans were extracted from the *Accreditation Self-Study* report and articulate the library's intention to study further service options:

1. Identify the impact of new technologies on staffing, equipment, resources, and supplies, and present special needs requests within the budget process
2. Present strategies to deal with these issues in the Technology Master Plan
3. Provide Internet access to students
4. Continue to plan for extended dial-in/home access to PCC's learning resources to expand hours of service and access to resources
5. Design a plan to inform Library Board representatives of new developments in information technologies and information retrieval methods
6. Create native language audio tours for the library that correspond to foreign languages most commonly spoken in the PCC service communities
7. Study the library needs of students at the new Community Education Center and design a plan for off-campus library services
8. Explore cooperative borrowing agreements with nearby academic libraries such as Cal-State, LA

• *Staffing*

The library staff actively participates in the goal setting, decision making, and evaluation of services. Collectively, the staff comprises over *200* years of service to the college. Their dedication is great, their skills and expertise have been fine tuned, and their contributions are significant. Library staff function as effective team members and it is this process that provides avenues for personal growth and development of professional skills, but also increases the likelihood that library programs and activities will succeed. These are also goals that are consistent with the resources, community partnerships, and governance goals outlined in the College's educational master plan.

The following factors are significant when considering the dynamic transition to the new facility in 1993:
- ◆ Library's service area doubled
- ◆ Seating capacity doubled
- ◆ Circulation, exit counts, library instruction to classes and students rose dramatically

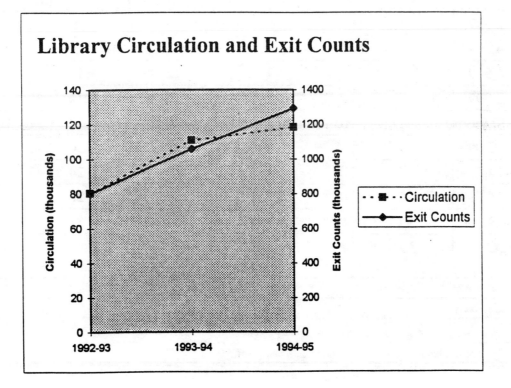

4

Library Instruction to Classes and Students

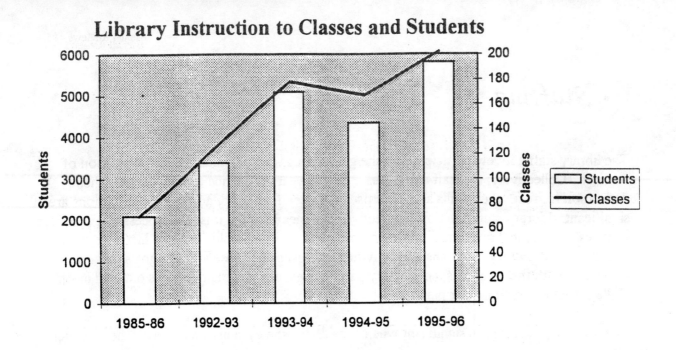

According to the Association of College and Research Libraries *Standards for Community, Junior, and Technical College Learning Resource Programs*, Shatford Library falls below the minimum, national standards for staffing for a library of its size. (This standard reflects only traditional library and media services.)

FTE Students	Administrators min. & excel.	Professional min.	excel.	Technicians min.	excel.	Other Staff min.	excel.	Total Staff min.	excel.
1,000- 2,999	1	3	5	3	6	3	6	10	18
3,000- 4,999	1	5	7	5	8	4	8	15	24
5,000- 6,999	1	7	9	7	12	6	11	21	33
7,000- 8,999	1	8	11	9	17	7	14	25	43
9,000-10,999	1	10	15	11	20	9	17	31	53
11,000-12,999	2	14	21	13	24	11	20	40	67
13,000-14,999	2	16	24	16	28	13	24	47	78
15,999-16,999	2	18	27	19	32	16	28	55	89
17,000-19,000	**2**	**20**	**30**	**21**	**36**	**18**	**32**	**61**	**100**
PCC	*1.25*[1]	*5.3*[2]		*10.52*[3]		*1.2*[4]		*18.71*	

[1]	Rod Foster, Mary Ann Laun
[2]	Librarians
[3]	Classified support staff and supervisors, Library and IRC
[4]	Secretaries (Jennifer Cooper (.69) and Imelda Martinez (.5)

The library recognizes that this standard is considered to be unrealistically high, yet benchmark comparisons with comparable institutions show that an augmentation of staff is needed to meet current service demands. (Note: Benchmarks were chosen based on the American Association of Community Colleges FTES largest single campus counts.)

Staffing Comparisons -- California Benchmarks
Community College Library and Media Services, 1995-1996

College	FTES credit	Librarians	Classified Staff	Total Staff
Pasadena City College	18,598[1]	6.3	10.5 Library: 6.83 Media: 3.69	16.8
El Camino College	16,158	5	14 Library: 12 Media: 2	19
Long Beach	16,495	7.6	9.5 Library: 7.5 Media: 2	17.1
Mt. San Antonio College	19,346	5.3	18 Library: 15 Media: 3	23.3
Santa Monica	16,595	6.75	11.5 Library: 6 Media: 5.5	18.25

[1] FTES figures are from 1994-95 Annual FTES (resident, nonresident and apprentice FTES) from San Joaquin Delta Community College District report *Financial Statistics for Current Cost of Education, 1994-95*

In order to have a true assessment of Shatford Library's staffing comparison with national standards, it is helpful to look at the reality of staffing in community college libraries outside of the state of California (see next page).

Staffing Comparisons -- Out of State Benchmarks
Community College Library and Media Services, 1995-1996

College	FTES credit	Librarians (FTE)	Classified Staff	Total Staff
Pasadena City College	**18,598**	**6.3**	**10.5** Library: 6.83 Media: 3.69	**16.8**
Lansing CC (Lansing, MI)	18,913	8	11 Library: 9 Media: 2	17
College of Du Page	16,000	10 (plus 2 FTE part-time)	38+ Library & Media combined: 38 (plus 30 part time classified positions)	48+
Nassau CC (Garden City, NY)	15,000	14 (plus 19 part time working 4-20 hours/week)	20 Library: 18 Media: 2	34+
Community College of Philadelphia	11,200	7	17 Library: 9 Media: 8	24
Sinclair CC (Dayton, OH)	10,109	9	9 Library & Media combined: 9	18
William Raney Harper College (Palatine, IL)	7,000	6	16 Library: 11 Media: 5	22

The Library recognizes due to the high volume of students and heavy use of the collection and services that planning for augmentations in staffing is a critical factor in the delivery of library services. The Library has addressed staffing issues within the budget process this year and also in the following *Accreditation Self-Study* recommendation: *"Submit to the Budget Committee a five year staffing plan which will provide adequate professional and classified staff for the present and will meet the future increasing and fast changing demands in the information technology arena."*

• *Collections*

The following factors are significant when considering the evolution of the library's budget and the corresponding rapid rate of inflation of book and periodical prices:

- The library's budget has remained static over the last 10 years with the exception of a special augmentation from the state in 1987 and PCC Foundation funding in 1994-1998
- The average cost of U.S. college books has risen from $31.19 (1985) to $48.17 (1995), *a 54%. increase*
- The average cost of U.S. periodicals has risen from $86.10 (1985) to $149.46 (1995); *a 86% increase*
- The library's collection is an aging one, due to a static budget and the increasing prices of library resources
- The library did not receive a special augmentation from the state ($1,000,000) as anticipated when the new building was completed

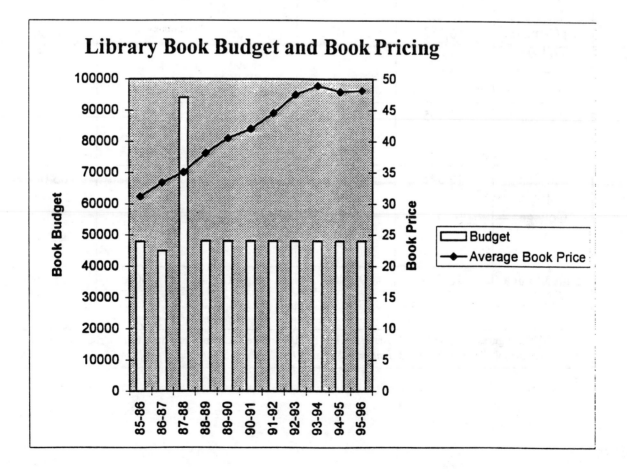

Source: *Bowker Annual of Library and Book Trade Almanac*

Collection and Budget Comparisons -- California Benchmarks
Community College Library and Media Services, 1995-1996

College	FTES Credit[1]	Volumes in Library	Book Budget	Periodical Subscriptions	Periodical Budget
Pasadena City College	18,598	115,000	48,000 (reflects 18,000 for network subscriptions) (plus Foundation augmentation of $50,000)	500	41,000
El Camino College	16,158	115,000	110,000 (includes 18,000 for CD-ROM subscriptions)	870	50,000
Long Beach	16,495	148,534	68,000	389	37,700
Mt. San Antonio College	19,346	88,345	53,000	756	65,000
Santa Monica	16,595	99,000	58,000	500	25,000

[1] FTES figures are from 1994-95 Annual FTES (resident, nonresident and apprentice FTES) from San Joaquin Delta Community College District report *Financial Statistics for Current Cost of Education, 1994-95*

Collection and Budget Comparisons -- Out-of-State Benchmarks

College	FTES Credit	Volumes in Library	Book Budget	Periodical Subscription	Periodical Budget
Pasadena City College	**18,598**	**115,000**	**48,000** (plus Foundation augmentation of $50,000)	**500**	**41,000**
Lansing Community College (Lansing, MI)	18,913	110,000	80,000 (plus 140,000 for media, standing orders, CD-ROM)	600	40,000
College of Du Page (Glen Ellen, IL)	16,000	156,000	230,000 (plus 60,000 for electronic media)	1,000	93,000
Nassau CC (Garden City, NY)	15,000	183,000	128,000 (plus 32,000 for media)	796	110,000
Sinclair CC (Dayton, OH)	10,109	135,000	180,000	678	93,000
Community College of Philadelphia	11,200	100,000	141,000	550	45,000
William Raney Harper College (Palatine, IL)	7,000	110,000	159,000	850	143,000

The Library recognizes the critical need for budget augmentations for collections and has documented this need through the budget process this year. In addition, the following *Accreditation Self-Study* recommendations address collection issues:

1. Identify ways to defray the supplies and subscriptions costs for electronic resources
2. Explore more options for involving more faculty in library materials selection and evaluations
3. Design a plan to inform Library Board Representatives of new developments in information technologies and information retrieval methods.

Summary

As Pasadena City College faces the challenges of today's diverse societies and information needs, connections between all segments of the college community are the springboards for meeting the college's educational mission and goals.

As the Shatford Library moves forward with its program planning, it is important to articulate clearly the connections between service, staffing and collection resources that are needed to support student's needs in their pursuit of learning. It is also essential to consider the numerous economic factors that play significant roles in the Library's program planning.

Appendix 1

Shatford Library User Survey, 1995

1. How often do you use the PCC Shatford Library?
A.	daily or weekly	46%
B.	monthly	21%
C.	rarely	30%
D.	never	3%

2. Generally, when looking for information in the Shatford Library, do you find information that you need?
A.	yes	56%
B.	no	7%
C.	partially	36%

3. If you answered "no" or "partially", indicate the most common reason.
A.	Couldn't find any information	17%
B.	Information I needed was checked out or not available (missing, overdue, not on the shelf, etc.)	45%
C.	Other	37%

4. When you find information, how would you characterize it?
A.	current	33%
B.	too old	23%
C.	just right	44%

5. How would you describe the *quantity* of the information you find in the library?
A.	too little	35%
B.	too much	6%
C.	the right amount for my needs	58%

6. How would you describe the *quality* of the information you find in the library?
A.	too difficult or too scholarly	10%
B.	appropriate level	80%
C.	too easy or too popular	10%

7. What is your most common use of the library?
A.	class assignments	64%
B.	personal interests	10%
C.	job related interests	2%
D.	study hall	21%
E.	Other	3%

8. Do you feel that the library is open long enough to meet your needs?
A.	yes	57%
B.	no	29%
C.	no opinion	14%

9. Do you feel comfortable asking the librarian for assistance?
A.	yes	67%
B.	no	15%
C.	no opinion	18%

10. If no, why not?
A.	I like to help myself	22%
B.	The librarian is too busy	21%
C.	I don't know where the librarian is	11%
D.	I am afraid to ask for help	8%
E.	Other	38%

11. Do you feel comfortable using the the computers in the library?
A.	yes	72%
B.	no	17%
C.	no opinion	11%

12. How do you rate the library's computerized book catalog?
A.	easy to use	44%
B.	neither easy nor difficult	43%
C.	difficult to use	13%

13. How do you rate the electronic indexes of magazines and journals?
A.	easy to use	38%
B.	neither easy nor difficult	47%
C.	difficult to use	15%

14. In general, how do you rate the library's services?
A.	excellent	17%
B.	good	59%
C.	fair	22%
D.	poor	2%

Survey participants: 1,285

Pasadena City College

Appendix 2

Titles by Publication Year
1940-1996

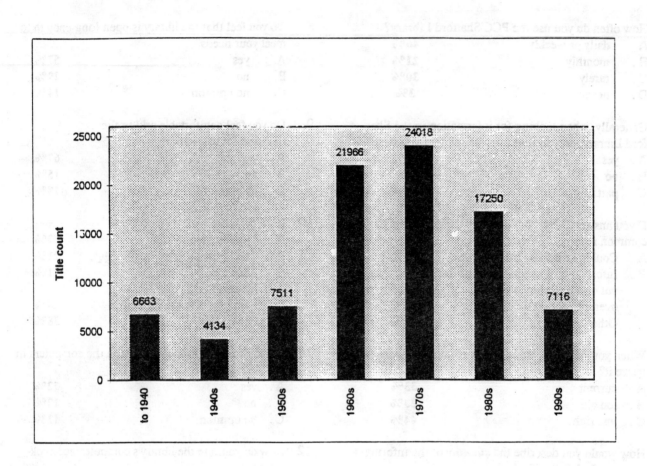

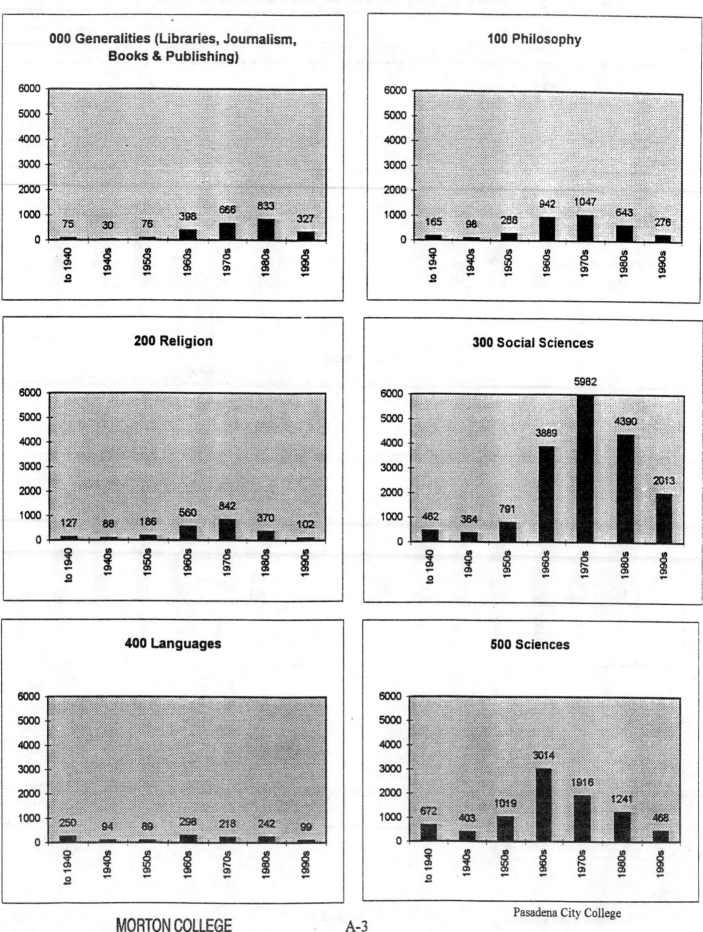

000 Generalities (Libraries, Journalism, Books & Publishing)

to 1940	1940s	1950s	1960s	1970s	1980s	1990s
75	30	76	398	666	833	327

100 Philosophy

to 1940	1940s	1950s	1960s	1970s	1980s	1990s
165	98	286	942	1047	643	276

200 Religion

to 1940	1940s	1950s	1960s	1970s	1980s	1990s
127	88	186	560	842	370	102

300 Social Sciences

to 1940	1940s	1950s	1960s	1970s	1980s	1990s
462	364	791	3889	5982	4390	2013

400 Languages

to 1940	1940s	1950s	1960s	1970s	1980s	1990s
250	94	89	298	218	242	99

500 Sciences

to 1940	1940s	1950s	1960s	1970s	1980s	1990s
672	403	1019	3014	1916	1241	468

Pasadena City College

Appendix 3
Titles by Subjects Areas and Publication Year

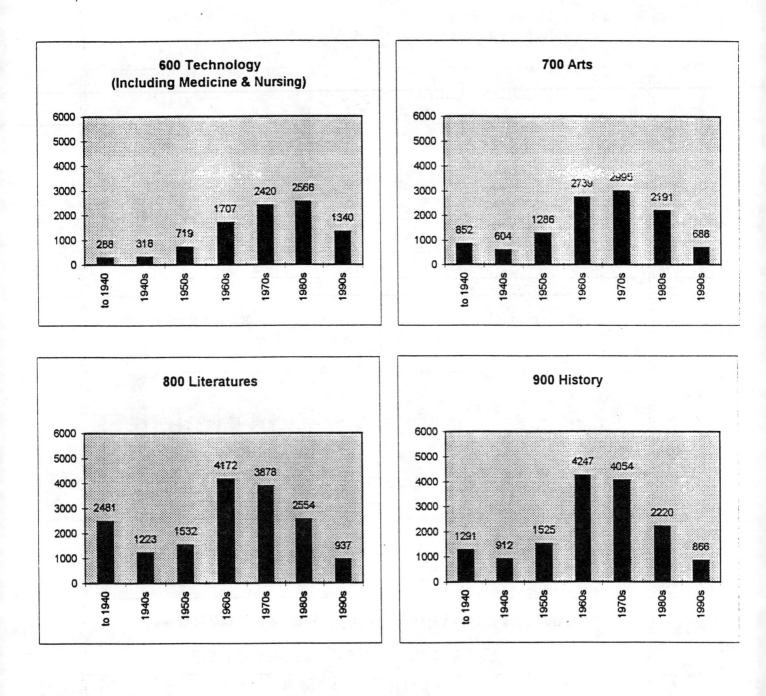

Cañada College Library

Internal Program Review, Planning, and Budgeting 1997-1998

Cañada College Library

Annual Self-Assessment, Planning, Budgeting
for
1997-1998

TABLE OF CONTENTS

Overview of Program 1996-1997

Annual Statistics

Cañada College Library
Overview of Program 1996-1997

During the current academic year, Cañada College Library has continued its efforts to work supportively with campus instructional programs. Because our district has a strong commitment to using technology in the curriculum our library is able to offer a range of resources. A reference librarian is updating Learning Center course material so that our students will more effectively learn how to use these electronic library resources. Among the resources acquired this year the library added a second Internet workstation, dial-up access to the computer catalog and a collection of four full-text periodical databases. Unfortunately, we have not increased the number of patron workstations. With the anticipated donation of computers from the Business and Social Sciences Division, however, we project that five additional workstations will be available to students and faculty in the Fall Semester.

Approximately fifty classes visited the library for orientations. This gave hundreds of students the opportunity to meet our staff, become familiar with our many resources and to have a pressure-free experience searching electronic resources. We are pleased that classes came from every academic division as well as counseling and psychological services. Hands on exercises, tailored to curriculum topics, were continually developed by librarians in consultation with faculty.

Although the library's budget was reduced this year, we received a $10,000 allocation from the Instructional Equipment/Library materials block grant. Books will be purchased with half of that amount and the remainder will be used to purchase media. Every effort was made to secure faculty input, particularly regarding the selection of videos. This section of the library is weak while faculty demand is strong. Recommended videos in Sociology, Interior Design, Foreign Language, Literature, Engineering and other subjects are presently on order. Librarians are currently evaluating demonstration copies of CD-ROM products, since we plan to purchase a major reference resource on CD-ROM. The library's highest priority is acquisition of a full-text newspaper index.

Each year the staff targets subjects for improvement. This year we purchased many books for the science, medicine and technology collections. To accommodate the need for materials in English as a second language, we purchased approximately one-hundred titles (recommended by English Institute faculty) for a collection that was established two years ago. The library also continues to benefit from generous donations. Most notably, the Early Childhood Education program regularly contributes books and videos. The library now houses and circulates the program's Safe Start collection of games, puppets and dolls. Our library further benefits from the profits of an ongoing used book sale that our Circulation Desk staff manages. We keep college faculty updated on our collection by publishing bibliographies such as our New Acquisitions and Periodical Holdings lists.

Finally, to keep abreast of library and information technology trends, all members of the library staff engage in formal and informal professional development activities. We believe the library program, which consists of services, staff and resources significantly contributes to the teaching, learning and student success to which this campus aspires.

Cañada College Library
Annual Statistics

Collection Expenditures

CATEGORY	1993-94	1994-95	1995-96
Reference Books	$ 5,866.00	$ 2,639.00	$ 3,456.00
Periodicals - Print and CD-ROM Subscriptions	14,237.00	15,103.00	14, 314
Other Contract Svcs.	NA	NA	3,200.00
Books	1,172.00	3,820.00	1,062.00
Videos	NA	400.00	252.00
TOTAL	$ 21,275.00	$ 23,033.00	$ 22,.284.00

Collection Holdings

ACTIVITY	1993-94	1994-95	1995-96
Volumes Added	153	531	296
Volumes Withdrawn	337	143	493
Total Volumes Held	45,902	46,290	46,236
Periodicals:			
Print Subscriptions	142	156	143
Microfilm	10	10	11
Online Full-Text	86	86	196
TOTAL SUBSCRIPTIONS	238	252	350
Videos	296	324	341

Library Services

ACTIVITY	1993-94	1994-95	1995-96
FTE Enrollment	3,601	3,514	3,449
Hours Open per Week	60	60 (Fall) 56.5 (Spring)	60 (Fall) 56.5 (Spring
Classes in Library	10	18	14
Number of Students	184	354	203
Class Orientations	43	49	53
Number of Students	845	946	1014
Total Classes	53	67	67
Total Students	1029	1,300	1217
Reference Questions Answered	4,042	4,290	3,616
Circulation	7,255	7,858	8,514
Circulation of Reserves & Videos	1,516	1,905	1,694
New Patrons Registered	111	136	82
Cañada Registration Count	287	479	557
Average Daily Attendance	237	277	234

Cañada College Library

1997-98 INTERNAL SELF-ASSESSMENT, PLANNING, BUDGETING DOCUMENT
April 28, 1997

PROGRAM PHILOSOPHY

The primary responsibility of Cañada College Library is to support the instructional program priorities of teaching, learning and student success in the context of a multicultural environment. The library strives to ensure that all persons in Cañada's learning community become skilled in the selection and use of research tools and technologies as well as skilled in the exploration of ideas. Cañada College Library further strives to inspire students and faculty to become independent researchers and life long library users.

ASSESSMENT OF 1996-1997 PROGRAM GOALS AND OBJECTIVES

Maintaining the established level of library service to patrons amidst numerous staff and technology changes was the main challenge facing us this year. Adjusting to staff fluctuations was the most difficult challenge because over the two semesters we introduced five new librarians and each worked fewer hours than previous librarians. Similarly, we added a number of new electronic resources but had fewer workstations upon which to use them. This problem was exacerbated by hardware failures and computer technician understaffing.

Canada College

Goal I: Develop information resources by providing collections
          that ensure current information of sufficient depth,
          breadth and relevance to the curriculum.

   Objective A: Further expand, while also weeding
                  periodical, pamphlet, book and video collections in
                  selected areas: science & technology, language and
                  literature.

**Librarians carefully weeded worn, outdated or mutilated materials
in these subject areas: medicine, literature and general and
European history. Additional weeding in agriculture, botany and
zoology is planned for this semester.   It is library policy to
consult faculty before books are discarded.**

**To date, three hundred fifty-eight (358) volumes were added to
the collection.   Approximately 40% of these are in the area of
science, technology and medicine and 22% in language and
literature.   These volumes are in addition to the 1996 Groliers
Multimedia Encyclopedia on CD-ROM, and the 1996 Encyclopedia
Americana.**

   Objective B: Increase subject specific full-text databases
                  and CD-ROM reference tools in above mentioned areas.

**The library now subscribes to the four full-text online
periodical databases and their backfiles: Academic ASAP, Business
and Company ASAP, General Reference Center and Health Reference
Center.   We also now subscribe to the National Newspaper Index
which locates citations for the New York Times, Wall Street**

Journal, Washington Post, Los Angeles Times and Christian Science Monitor. Patrons now have remote access to these databases also.

Objective C: Dedicate second opac to Internet access.

A new pentium pc loaded with Netscape Navigator and Microsoft Explorer offers public access to the Internet. The library's policy on Internet use is regularly updated.

Goal II: Promote instructional and research services to patrons individually as well as in groups.

Objective A: Library staff will actively exchange program ideas in campus committees -- Curriculum   Committee, Canada Computer Committee, Associated Students and Instruction Council.

Staff participation in campus committees is irregular because the library cannot be left unsupervised.   However, a library representative attends every All College Meeting, Facilities Planning and BAS/LR Division meeting.

Objective B: Develop bibliographic instruction options for Science, Language and Literature.

Tailored library workshops were presented to chemistry, ESL, career planning, reading classes and English literature.

Objective C: Create library pathfinders and orientation exercises in collaboration with faculty and Learning Center staff.

A number of new and updated guides were prepared by librarians to assist in student mastery of constantly evolving electronic research tools. They range from the systemwide online library

3

catalog to the Internet.   In order to upgrade the Learning Center's self-paced research courses a reference librarian is working with Sharon Pastori, Learning Center Coordinator.

Goal III: Continue professional development opportunities for
        library staff.

    Objective A: Provide flexible scheduling for attendance at
        training sessions, professional workshops and classes.

Mary Huzarewicz successfully completed two courses in Library Technology at Foothill College: *Introduction to Library Skills* and *Technical Processing: Cataloging and Processing* and also attended the PLS/SBCLS Library Paraprofessional Conference workshops.   She is a member of ALA (American Library Association), COLT (Council of Library Technicians) and the Friends of the Redwood City Library. She subscribes to four (4) library related listservs.

Carol Moseley, Senior Library Media Technician, completed two semesters of business computing Office Professional and Word 6.0 and has subscribed to the Library Support Staff listserv.

Marilyn Hayward, Coordinator of Library Services attended the League for Innovation in the Community College 1996 Conference on Information Technology, and completed several courses in the SFSU Multimedia Studies Program. She holds membership in several professional organizations and subscribes to three library related listservs as well as print journals.

Objective B: Participate in SMCCCD and PLS staff
           development activities.

As adjunct faculty members, all part-time librarians participate in Flex Day workshops. *Using Powerpoint*, *Developing Your Own Web Page* and the workshop *Collaborating, Critical Thinking and Diversity* are among those they attended.

Carol Moseley and Mary Lou Huzarewicz attended the April 18 classified staff retreat.   Carol also attended the Flex Day workshop titled *Skyline's New "Electronic" Library*.

Marilyn Hayward attended two Center for Teaching and Learning (CTL) sponsored workshops and the Peninsula Library System Technology Retreat held in January.   In January she also attended the SMCCCD Office of Personnel Services' Management Institute.

Objective C: Maintain institutional membership in Learning
           Resources Association of California Community Colleges
           (LRACCC) and Council of Chief Librarians (CCL).

Cañada College Library's memberships are still current.

Goal IV: Contribute to planning of new library facility.
     Objective A: Staff will participate in SMCCCD committees
The Coordinator, both Senior Library/Media Technicians and hourly librarians contribute to the activities related to SMCCCD Facilities Planning.

Objective B: Staff will survey library literature, attend
library planning workshops and consult with
knowledgeable professionals.

Using electronic library resources, library literature concerning
the building and/or remodeling of library facilities has been
retrieved and circulated to staff members.   The library also
purchased books on the topic that were published by the American
Library Association.   In addition, the library coordinator has
engaged in in-person as well as online discussions of library
facilities with librarians and library coordinators.

Objective C: Staff will tour nearby college libraries.

The library coordinator has made numerous visits to the newly
constructed Skyline College Library and College of San Mateo's
renovated facility.   As mentioned previously, Senior
Library/Media Technician Carol Moseley attended the Skyline
College Library Flex Day workshop.

1997-1998 Cañada College Library Program Goals

Goal I: Develop information resources by providing collections that ensure current information of sufficient depth, breadth and relevance to the curriculum.

Objective A: Further expand, while also weeding periodical, pamphlet, book and video collections in selected areas: science & technology, language and literature.

Objective B: Add a full-text newspaper index on CD-ROM.

Objective C: Increase the number of computer workstations in order to expand student access to information resources.

Goal II: Promote instructional and research services to patrons individually as well as in groups.

Objective A: Library staff will actively exchange program ideas in campus committees -- Curriculum   Committee, Canada Computer Committee, Associated Students and Instruction Council.

Objective B: Develop bibliographic instruction options for Science, Language and Literature.

Objective C: Create library pathfinders and orientation exercises in collaboration with faculty and Learning Center staff.

Goal III: Continue professional development opportunities for
library staff.

Objective A: Provide flexible scheduling for attendance at
training sessions, professional workshops and classes.

Objective B: Participate in SMCCCD and PLS staff
development activities.

Objective C: Maintain institutional membership in Learning
Resources Association of California Community Colleges
(LRACCC) and Council of Chief Librarians (CCL).

Goal IV: Fill the vacant reference librarian position.

Goal V: Contribute to planning of remodeled and expanded
library facility.

Objective A: Staff will participate in SMCCCD committees

Objective B: Staff will survey library literature, attend
library planning workshops and consult with
knowledgeable professionals.

Objective C: Staff will tour at least one nearby college
or public library.

1995-98 LIBRARY SERVICE GOALS

Activity	Goal 95-96	Actual 95-96	Goal 96-97* (+5%)	Goal 97-98* (+5%)
Daily Gate Count	291	234	246 *	259*
Circulation	8,250	8,514	8,940 *	9,411*
Reserve Circulation	2,000	1,694	1,779 *	1,873*
Hours Open Per Week	56.5	Fall 60 Spr. 56.5	52.5	52.5
Class Visits	70	67	70	74
Ref. Quest.	4,505	3,616	3,797	3,997

1995-98 STAFFING GOALS

	Actual 95-96	Goal 96-97	Actual 96-97	Goal 97-98
Admin. FTE	1 (11 mos.)	1 (11 mos.)	1 (11 mos.)	1 (11 mos.)
FT Librarian	0		0	1
Adjt. FTE	1.44	2	Fall 1.38 Spring 1.36	1
Class. FTE	2	2	1 (12 mos.) 1 (11 mos.)	2
Stu. Asst.	600 hrs	630 hrs	(570 max.)	570

Canada College

1995-98   BUDGET GOALS

	Expended FY 96	Allocated FY 97	Expended FY 97	Requested FY 98
Acct 4110 Ref. Bks.	3,456.00	1,600.00	3565.00	3,200.00
Acct 4510 Misc. Supp.	942.54	600.00	1575.00	1,000.00
Acct 4513 Subscriptions	14,313.90	8,000.00	12,081.00	11,000.00
Acct 4580 Centr. Dup.	283.00	233.00	233.00	233.00
Acct 5220 Mileage	0	100.00	0	
Acct 5310 Dues/Mber.	75.00	0	75.00	100.00
Acct 5630 Repair Eq.	0	0	300.00	
Acct 5690 Other Ctr.	3,200.00	3,600.00	554.00	600.00
Acct 6310 Books	1,062.56	6,000.00	1,750.00	4,000.00
TOTAL	**23,333.00**	**20,133.00**	**20,133.00**	**20,133.00**

1997-98 FACILITIES & EQUIPMENT REQUEST

Facilities:
1. Repair or replace automatic entry doors for ADA
2. Replace Reading Room carpet $15,750
3. Install ADA compliant Circulation Desk   3,150
4. Cable installation and Dynix license
    for mobile multimedia workstation   2,000
5. Periodical display racks   500

Equipment:

1. Personal computers 6 @ 2,500   15,000
2. Computer printers   6 @   300   1,800
3. LCD overhead projector   3,500
4. Mobile computer workstation   400
5. Projection screen   300
6. Microform reader/printer   3,500
7. Typewriter   500

Library And Learning Resources
PROGRAM REVIEW 1997

Source Documents

Acquisitions • Archives • Automation • Cataloging • Circulation • Periodicals
Reference and Bibliographic Instruction • User Surveys

▲

Alice Statler Library • Downtown Campus Library • John Adams Campus Library
Southeast Campus Library • Teachers Resource Center

City College of San Francisco

NUNEZ COMMUNITY COLLEGE
REVIEW FOR NON-INSTRUCTIONAL UNITS
LIBRARY SERVICES

I. **Unit Purpose Statement:** Provide a succinct unit mission statement and/or statement of purpose. The statement should be congruent with the College's statement of purpose and should provide a framework for the goals and objectives of the unit by addressing the desired outcomes of the educational, research, and/or service activities of the unit.

It is the mission of Nunez Community College Library to provide the library resources and services required to support the mission and goals of NCC. This is published in the Library Policies and Procedures Manual and expands to objectives and functions. (Attachment A)

II. **Unit Programs and Services**

    A.   Provide an organizational chart for your unit (Human Resources can help with this).

(Attachment B)

    B.   Major functions and services

        1.   List the major functions and services within the unit.

1) Selection and acquisition of materials, 2) Cataloging and maintenance of materials, 3) Individual and group instruction and reference assistance, 4) Provision and maintenance of computer databases, 5) Cooperative agreements and distance learning agreements, 6) Circulation of materials.

        2.   What services or functions which currently exist could be discontinued or transferred to another unit?

Collection of fine money could be transferred to the Business Office. This would have to be worked on for all the details. Have outside funding source for law library upkeep.

        3.   What services/functions are needed which do not currently exist?

We want to be accessible to the general public and as such are working on an agreement to house the St. Bernard Genealogical Society collection.

        4.   Draw a flow chart that shows the dynamic interactions among current functions, services and personnel. The unit head should be able to provide this information.

Flow chart attached. (Attachment C)

C.   Chart the volume of service for the last year provided in whatever ways are appropriate to the unit's function (e.g., calls, visits, appointments, projects, dollars, books/equipment checked out, programs, activities, transactions, referrals, work orders, etc.) Examples: 50 calls per week, 10 projects per semester, 6 work order per day.

These are for FY 96 - From IPEDS Report:

Circulation: 11,250	Average Weekly Gate Count: 1668
Reserves: 206	Average Weekly Reference Transactions: 228
ILL Received: 18	New books cataloged: 1174
BI Presentations: 61 to 704 People	

D.   What external developments and trends (such as legislation, demographic, professional practices) do you believe will have the greatest impact on the unit's programs, services, and operation?

Increased automation will affect the form of information provided by the library. More involvement with LOUIS and like consortia for improved service, but less individual control.

E.   Evaluation

    1.   On a scale of 1-10, how would you describe the level of functioning (effectiveness, efficiency) of this unit at this time? Please explain your rating.

8 - We are a highly effective and efficient unit as is demonstrated in our evaluations. We are hindered by a lack of space and manpower (especially now with no Director) in doing the best at everything. Cataloging in particular needs better tools to work efficiently in an automated environment.

    2.   Describe how you evaluate the success of your unit.

1 - Annual user survey in Spring. 2 - BI evaluations each semester. 3 - Written & verbal compliments and complaints from other departments (i.e., business inventory) and individuals. 4 - Increased usage (# of BI, circulation, patrons per day). 5 - Comparison of catalog to other institutions.

    a.   What are the unit's expected outcomes for general everyday responsibilities and how are they assessed?

Accurate circulation of materials 1, 4, 3
Helpful BI & reference assistance 1, 2, 4, 3
Accurate cataloging of materials 3, 4, 5
Provision of appropriate atmosphere for patrons 1, 2, 3, 4

b.   How do you respond to and incorporate recommendations and/or complaints from clientele (students, co-workers)?

Discuss at staff meetings or informally with affected staff members. Decide if changes need to be made and then implement them as soon as is feasible. Also, study problems and look for trends.

3.   Describe the results of outcome assessments over the past five years (Close that Loop!).

a.   What were the minimal acceptable standards used to judge performance?

For acquisitions, we use the ACRL guidelines. For other goals we determine if it has been done.

b.   What changes have been made as the result of assessments?

Changed hours, member of LOUIS, increased video holdings, increased number of books students can check out, built group study room, better control on getting circulating items returned, give holds to Student Services rather than business.

c.   What changes, if any, remain to be made as the result of those assessments?

Increase automation of cataloging, increase space for study areas.

4.   Has the unit undergone a major external evaluation in the last five years?

a.   If yes, describe the major findings.

SACS found the library to be in compliance with all "MUST" statements with the understanding that a new facility would be in place for Fall 1998. It was suggested that the library consult with the nursing faculty concerning the medical collection.

b.   If yes, what changes have been or will be made as the result of the findings?

The Acquisitions librarian (currently vacant) will consult with the nursing faculty to establish an appropriate collection. This has been noted in the 97-98 budget.

     c.   If no, what plans regarding external evaluation are being developed?

We also try to match the standards set by the Association of Colleges and Research Libraries (ACRL) for like institutions.

F.   Compared to similar units in comparable colleges:

     1.   What are the special strengths of the unit?

We are very patron oriented and go out of our way to give personalized attention. The staff works together very well - good communication across all areas.

     2.   What are the major weaknesses or deficiencies of the unit?

Lack of space, proper automation of cataloging, lack of professional staff.

G.   What direction do you believe the unit must take to be more successful within the next five years?

Move into the new facility, continue to upgrade computers every year, hire more staff (especially professional or at least experienced).

III.   Goals, Objectives, and Assessments

A.   List your unit's goals and objectives from the prior year's plan and give the status of each (or provide copies of your Action Plan and Outcomes Reports from your binder).

Goals and objectives of prior year are attached. (Attachment D)

B.   What are the major goals and objectives for your unit over the next five years? For example, areas such as service, teaching, research, student outcomes, program development and human, physical, and financial resources can be addressed.

New building, increase cataloging automation, increase community bond, better communications with faculty.

C.   . Describe how these goals and objectives relate to the next higher organizational level and to the Mission and Purpose of the College as a whole.

The library is part of Academic Affairs which is responsible for the education of the students. The more effective the library is, the better educated the students will be. Faculty communication is a key to student use.

IV.   **Human Resources**

A.   Staffing

1.   Discuss successes and/or difficulties and problems in recruitment and retention of staff. Include how ethnic and gender diversity in the unit is addressed.

It is difficult to get appropriate civil service employees for the paraprofessional positions. Libraries are lumped with the general clerical duties, but they are not the same. We are blessed to have found Doreen and Jean who don't fit this mold, but have not had success with filling other positions. We are ethnically and genderly diversified without making that an issue.

2.   Is the unit adequately staffed? If not, please explain.

There are currently two vacant positions - Director and Cataloging paraprofessional. As stated in the 97 Outcomes, there is also a need for another 1/2 time professional. If all those were filled, we would be adequately staffed.

3.   Prioritize the unit's unmet human resources needs.

1 - Director - This needs to be filled soon. This person previously did acquisitions as well which needs to be addressed.

2 - The other two positions are both helpful and could be filled in either order depending upon the right person coming along.

Elaine P. Nunez Community College

B.   Personnel Development Training

    1.   Describe the personnel development and training program in the unit.

Everyone attends various training each year through civil service, LOUIS, and/or other library related conferences. Employees are encouraged to attend these sessions during work hours. IAP's include development plans and outcomes.

    2.   List personnel development activities in the unit over the past five years.

Various civil service training (paraprofessionals), Many LOUIS training sessions for NOTIS and databases (both), Library conferences (librarians), Computer software seminars (both).

    3.   Are personnel development opportunities adequate?

Adequate - yes, but with constant budget cuts, I see them becoming scarce. Particularly the ability to go to out of state conferences and training (time is also a factor - when there are so few staff, going to training means everyone else has to work harder).

    4.   Prioritize the unmet development and training needs.

With increased technology, all librarians should be able to go to an out of state conference or training session each year (SOLINET in Atlanta, NOTIS Users Group in Chicago, ACRL Convention).

C.   Morale

    1.   On a scale of 1-10, rate the morale in the unit. Explain the rating.

8 - I think there are always times when morale gets hit particularly when we are understaffed. It is easy to get discouraged when confronted with piles of work, but as a group we work well together.

I can't speak for my colleagues. However, my morale would improve it the functions of my department were automated in a fashion commensurate with peer institutions in the LOUIS consortium. Automating cataloging function would free me up to handle other areas of my job description more efficiently. Otherwise, I'm content with my work environment, my colleagues, and my duties and I like working with the students. Rating - 7.

8 - It is frustrating at times to get the kind of student workers we desire to work in the library. However, the staff always works together in the best interest of the library and of each other and I enjoy working here.

I have to give this job a 10. I like the students and the staff is A-1. I'm content with my work.

8 - The staff works well together. We can wear each others' shoes. This does make one stretched out because we are understaffed in certain areas. The job does get done when we all work together.

2.   What do you do to foster positive morale and address concerns?

Be open to comments/complaints. Address those as mentioned in IIE 2B. Keep a good attitude and be sure everyone is pulling his/her own weight. Give everyone a stake in ownership.

V.   Physical Resources

A.   Equipment/Technology

1.   List equipment technology in the unit.

Networked computers with Internet access for offices and patrons, LOUIS access for Library Management System and databases, CD-ROM tower for networked access, modem for ILL, coin operated photo copier for patrons, networked printer for patrons, laser and ink jet printers for staff, microform readers and reader/printers, media equipment for in library use and circulation to faculty and staff on campus, VCR tape duplicating machinery.

2.   Is the equipment/technology adequate? If not, please explain.

Yes, it is adequate at the moment thanks to the LOUIS grant. However, there are still some outdated computers that need replacing. We also need a staff photo copier and FAX machine which were taken to Port Sulphur. The VCR tape duplicating machine is dying.

3.   Prioritize the unfunded equipment/technology needs.

The photo copier and FAX are merely replacing what we always had. There are Port Sulphur's expenses. The VCR duplicating machine is mainly used for telecourses and is a distance learning expense. The library should acquire 1-2 computers each year just to replace outdated equipment.

Elaine P. Nunez Community College

B.   . Facilities

    1.   List and describe the offices and work spaces currently allocated to the unit.   (information on square footage is available from Institutional Research)

5000 square feet in several connecting rooms: Main, Reference, Law, Periodical, 3 offices, workroom, archives, media room, study room and listening room.

    2.   Does this physical space meet the unit's present needs?

No! It is far too small. These will be met in the new building which will be 24,000 square feet.

3. If not, what specific change(s) in the location, configuration, condition, and/or space would satisfy these needs? Prioritize these requirements.

Technical services in an enclosed area, space on the shelves for books, climate control for archives, study areas for individuals and groups, classroom for BI.

VI. Financial Resources

A. Budget

1. Chart the budget and expenditures for the unit as a whole and for major subunits over the past five years.

The proposed budgets for each year are included as well as the actual budgets for most years. As far as matching up with expenditures that is one of the problems we have. It makes planning difficult. (Attachment E)

2. Is the budget adequate? If not, please explain.

So far, we have been able to obtain necessary items. However, it is tightening which is difficult on a library since we need to continue to acquire new materials consistently. Without grants, we would be in big trouble. (See VII C)

3. Prioritize the unfunded needs that have not been listed previously.

---

4. Study the unit's goals and chart the projected budget by year through the planning period (5 years). Chart the upcoming fiscal year in detail. Estimate years two through five of the planning period.

Proposed budget attached for FY 98. Our budget will increase over the next five years when we move to the new building. Otherwise, there will be little change from the proposed budget for FY 98' (as opposed to the actual). (Attachment F)

.

B.   .External Sources of Funds

    1.   How many student workers are designated to the unit and how are they funded? (federal or state)?

Federal - 3 - We also pay for our library clerk from state funds as a replacement for one student worker.

    2.   Are there any other workers in the unit funded by external, non-traditional sources? Explain.

One worker from the Council on Aging.

    3.   Indicate the amount of money the unit has received over the past five years from sources outside the College for programs, services, personnel, or equipment, in addition to that designated for student workers. Indicate uses to which these funds have been put (e.g. grants, development funds).

Friends of the Library $ 3183.64, LOUIS Grant $ 26,000, LEQSF Grant $ 8,000 (shared with Arts & Sciences), Dean Law Library $ 30,000 - $ 40,000 in kind, and UMI contest $ 10,000.

    4.   Indicate how these funds have been used.

Shelving for Law Library, Microfiche Reader/Printer, LOUIS Grand Opening, Range of shelving for oversize, computers & printers for LOUIS access, equipment for producing oral histories (shared with Arts & Sciences), backfiles of Times Picayune microfilm.

    5.   What are the unit's plans for seeking external sources of funding?

We continually search for grant funding and outside sources in the community.

VII.   Coordination with Other Units

A.   With which other units on campus does this unit interact on a regular basis? Describe the interactions.

Academic Divisions - work with faculty for collection development, bibliographic instruction; Business Department - purchase requests, inventory; Student Services - ID's, holds on students; Any department/administrator with library needs (especially AV equipment).

B.   What works well with these interactions? How are positive interactions fostered?

We try to keep the lines of communications open with each department, so the needs of all are fulfilled. We follow guidelines set up by them.

C.   What does not work? How would you suggest solving these problems? How do you address these problems?

The budget/actual process has been a problem that has been slowly improving. We continue to work with the Business department to provide what they need and get what we need in a timely manner and in a compatible form.

VIII.   **Comments** - Comment on any other aspects of the unit, its programs or services which you consider relevant to this review.

_____

_____

_____

Program: <u>Learning Resources:</u>
                 <u>Library & Media Services</u>
Prepared by: <u>All Faculty & Staff</u>
Recorded by: <u>K. Nakano at request of division</u>

1997-98
Edmonds Community College
ANNUAL PROGRAM REVIEW FOR INSTRUCTION

Note: Due to the inter-relatedness of the departments' requests, the Learning Resources Division chooses to write one report and has customized the Program Review form to address services provided to faculty/staff, the college, and students.

1. **What new information or important issues (if any) have emerged for your program in the past year that would have an impact on your allocation of resources? In your response please address the following indicators:**

a. Faculty/College/Student need/demand
What else for your departments should be considered when determining faculty/college/student need/demand?

RESPONSE:

<u>Library:</u>
The Library Campaign was 100% successful and was a long and dedicated effort. The Library remodel, begun in July 1997, will provide sorely needed collection growth space, a dedicated classroom, upgraded electrical and data infrastructure, better lighting, and more functional faculty and staff work areas. Reference and instructional space, media viewing space and individual and group study spaces have all been designed with students in mind. Unfortunately, the shelving and furniture costs were not thoroughly investigated at the beginning of the Library Campaign and the Library is now finding that it will not be able to buy all it needs with current Foundation funding. A private furniture vendor has quoted a $150,000 price tag for refurbished shelving and another $500,000 for enough carrels, study tables, media viewing stations and computer workstation furniture to meet the advertised doubling of seating from 250 to 500 seats. Furniture and shelving money was not set aside as part of the remodel project because at that time it was thought the Library Campaign monies would fully fund these purchases. A meeting of the Purchasing Officer and the Foundation Executive Director is planned as well as a later meeting with the President's Cabinet to determine the next steps. It is felt that as this was the College's first large scale foundation drive, it will be important to be sensitive to the feelings of donors who will expect a major installation of new furniture.

<u>Media Services:</u>
The number of faculty on the EdCC campus who make use of media and technology in the classroom continues to increase this year. Trailblazers among them have already completed multimedia-based learning modules that have become integral components of the learning process, and other faculty have begun to explore and learn about the possibilities from each another. Media Services has

worked closely with several faculty members in the planning and production of multimedia CD-ROMs. In some cases, faculty have spent their own time, money, and computer hardware and software resources in the development process and are now asking for college support of their efforts by making resources available to them in the classroom.

With Snohomish Hall's opening, Instructional Staff supported an "off-the-top" allocation this year to begin the installation of both basic and high-end technology in 11 classrooms ranging from overhead projectors on carts to data/video projectors mounted in the ceilings. Because most of the installations are in Snohomish Hall, it will be important to continue the installation of equipment in other classrooms across campus to provide opportunities for faculty in all departments to incorporate technology into their teaching.

b. **Changes in the external environment.** What external changes or trends may impact the department/program, such as changes in the economy, business employment opportunities, transfer requirements, etc.

RESPONSE:

Library:

Technological advances in accessing information continue to fuel the need for increased budgetary support of the library. Library resources are cheapest when bought through consortium pricing and the library must have adequate and available resources to make best use of its dollars as opportunities arise. For example, an Internet-available database subscribed to by one community college library may cost between $5,000 and $10,000 per year. The same database, when subscribed to as part of a consortium of libraries may cost as little as $2,000 a year. In addition, the development of databases is not stagnant and vendors continue to add depth, breadth and time coverage with new databases being developed each year.

Menu-driven systems in libraries are no longer the optimum way to find information: they require the student to know which particular database will meet their need; search through several menus to find the desired database; learn individual search software; and then if necessary, repeat the search in other databases.

The Library is currently investigating a web-based interface which would simultaneously search the EdCC library catalog, any other selected community college library catalog, and any selected periodical database. Such a system minimizes the need to repeat searches between databases and allows students to access information quickly and easily. Additionally, a web-based system would mean that faculty and students could access the system from any Internet-ready workstation, including classroom equipment for teaching purposes.

Budget-wise, the web-based system would require upgraded workstations to enable rapid transfer of results, including results from databases that have graphics, digital images and sound and video. In addition, higher-end locally situated and CTC-housed servers would be needed to support the system.

Media Services:
Media Services staff fill requests for satellite and cablecast tapings and also
schedule the growing number of requests for teleconferences from faculty, staff,
organizations and the community at large. The resources required to broadcast
EdCC telecourses over Channel 28 have increased as has the concomitant demand
from city councils to broadcast meetings and messages. Media Services is aware of
the important community relations role it plays in its provision of Channel 28
service, however its "start-up" nature has meant that the college must support
services rendered to the cities in order to garner future returns. The President is
aware of this situation and Media Services staff and the associate dean are working
with the cities for partial remuneration for staff time and equipment.

c. Unmet student learning needs. Other than staffing, space, and
equipment, what student learning needs are not currently met in your
department/.program.

Library and Media Services:
Both the library and media services departments must take action to insure that the
college-wide abilities are included wherever possible.

d. Other (if applicable).

2.   1998-99 FTEF request

RESPONSE:
No change is requested.

3.   Please list other budget-related requests that your program
anticipates at this time. **Please include justification.**

a. **Full-time faculty**

   X   No

b. **Full-time staff**

Position: Annual Salary:

Justification:

The following is a joint request from the library and media services
departments.

At the present time a minimum level of technical support is provided to the
library by a technical support staff from the Academic Computing department.
Learning Resources is required to pay a fee each year, currently $6,000, to have
this service provided since Academic Computing is a revenue-based operation.
This minimum support is no longer adequate and the dual charge to provide
support service for both the library and Academic Computing results in
conflicting priorities. No negative criticism is meant toward the staff member
who provides this service. The point is that it is simply not enough for what
needs to be done.

Both departments have seen a marked rise in the need for technical support for computer and media equipment in the last two years: the library because of its LAN and future web-based catalog, and media services because of its growing inventory of high-end classroom and TRC equipment.

After considering their needs, the library and media services departments therefore jointly request a **full-time classified position** to provide dedicated support for the equipment mentioned above. Ideally, each department would have its own technical support position, but we understand the budgetary implications and therefore are requesting the absolute minimum we need to provide services to students, faculty/staff, the college and the community.

Library Needs:
The library's current online catalog and combination of dial-up and CD-ROM based databases is a complex arrangement that requires many hours of dedicated technical support. Some smaller database vendors have not standardized on a platform that is compatible with the main menuing system and this creates a need for local programming to allow these databases to be accessed from the library's LAN. Many vendors update their search software on a quarterly or twice-yearly basis and it takes many hours of tweaking to have all databases working from a single station at the same time, let alone through a LAN.

The library is now investigating the feasibility of moving to a web-based search environment with web interface software written by the company who provides it with its online catalog software. While the actual programming will lessen, there will still be a great need for a technical support person to communicate with vendor representatives whenever problems arise. The library will also look to this support person to manage the actual migration from a LAN environment to a web environment.

Technical support is also needed by the library staff who manage the circulation and technical services systems, both of which are an integral part of information that is reflected in the library online catalog. Circulation staff depend on a system that works with both the mainframe located at CTC, the library LAN, and the college's EDPASS system. Problems can occur at many junctures and time and support staff are needed to troubleshoot and solve problems. Likewise, technical services staff also depend on clear lines to CTC and the library LAN and downtimes for both units impact their ability to provide current information to students on the collection and circulation status. Technical support is also needed by faculty and staff who service the reference desk to assist with downloading and printing problems faced by student users.

Media Services Needs:
Media Services began a classroom equipment installation project this year that we hope will continue in the future. High-end data/video projectors capable of projecting both computer data/graphics/images and video will require a support person who can assist when problems arise with computer hookups and playback. Although the current installation includes only two computers, it is thought that this trend will continue and support assistance will need to be in place to provide timely and knowledgeable assistance to faculty in the classroom.

Media Services will also need skilled support to assist with the College's growing commitment to distance education via telecourses and online courses.

In addition it is thought that the video server system, acquired through a grant by Information Technologies, will eventually fall to Media Services to staff and support as this could become primarily an instructional delivery system on the campus. Good technical support service will benefit those faculty members who rely on timely problem solving during a class period.

The two departments also believe they could learn much from a technical support person in order to do basic troubleshooting before calling for assistance. In this way, that staff member could also act as a trainer and resource person to the division so that all division faculty and staff could team up to provide the best services possible to students, faculty and staff.

It is the belief of the associate dean that the proposal for this minimum level of support for the two departments would find wide support among faculty and students. A working library LAN with accurate information and classroom equipment are primary resources that support the college's mission and goals and all will benefit from the creation of this position.

c. Space requests: (Please note, space requests will be reviewed by your dean/associate dean and forwarded to Instructional Staff and the Facilities Committee.)

What classroom changes, remodeling, or minor improvements are essential for the learning needs of your students? (Equipment requests will be considered during winter quarter.)

RESPONSE:

Library:
The roof of Lynnwood Hall leaks in windy weather and the brick walls are porous which results in inefficient heating and cooling and mold and mildew problems. With the remodel underway, the faculty and staff feel it is important to address these building issues in a timely manner.

Media Services:

Media Services did not benefit in either dollars or space from the library remodel or the Library Campaign. Media Services continues to move away from being just an equipment pool to a place where staff are dedicated to helping faculty integrate technology and media into their curriculums and classrooms.

Current Media Services staff and services spaces must be retained. Additional dedicated space is needed for the following functions:

- Video Lab/Editing Lab
  Primary Use: students
  Space Required: 2 rooms at 160 sq. ft. each

  Several instructors require students to video tape class assignments such as presentations, role play simulations and speeches. These rooms are needed for practice, videotaping and editing.

- Student TRC
  Primary Use: students
  Space Required: 1 room at 500 sq. ft.

  There is a growing demand for students to integrate multimedia into reports and presentations and there is currently no official place for students to produce this work. Media Services offers support and equipment use on a very limited basis. Several students are taking this request to the student government this year.

- Multipurpose Studio/Digital/Interactive Television Classroom
  Primary Use: faculty and students, secondary use for staff training
  Space Required: 1200 sq. ft.

  Currently Media Services staff spend 40 minutes for each videotaping request to transport, set-up and take-down equipment, not including the 50 minutes of classtime to assist in the videotaping in the classroom. The installations of classroom media equipment address only the showing of media, not the production of media. A large space adjacent to the media services staff areas is needed to better accommodate the growing number of requests with the same number of staff. This classroom could also be used as a training facility for faculty and staff in the use of technology in the classroom or workplace.

- Satellite and Interactive Television Conference Rooms
  Primarily Use: faculty/staff and community groups
  Space Required: 2 rooms needed: one to accommodate 20 persons and another to accommodate 40 persons

  Media Services and the secretary of Learning Resources jointly schedule faculty/staff and community requests for satellite downlinks, and teleconferences. The rooms need to be adjacent to Media Services to provide immediate assistance when necessary.

- Expanded TRC
  Primary Use: faculty/staff
  Space Required: additional 500 sq. ft. needed

  More space is needed to accommodate the various pieces of equipment needed for multimedia production including flatbed scanners, slide scanners, CD-ROM presses, printers, multiple monitors and audio equipment. Space is also required to allow for small groups to gather and work on projects together.

- Media Storage Space
  Primary Use: Media Services staff and student workers
  Space Required: 80 sq. ft. in every building

  Moving equipment from the central storage area in Mountlake Terrace requires time and is physically hard on equipment.

CENTRAL FLORIDA COMMUNITY COLLEGE
TACTICAL PLAN COMPONENT
Academic Year 1996-1997

INSTRUCTIONAL SUPPORT

Division/Department: **LEARNING RESOURCES CENTER**
Administrator: **Wanda Johnston**

STRATEGIC INSTITUTIONAL GOAL:

1. Improve and enlarge student access into programs (access refers to the opportunity to make use of all college facilities, programs and policies).

IDENTIFIED NEED:

Resources and services are needed to support, facilitate, and enhance informational and learning needs for CFCC students, faculty, staff, and other lifelong learners.

SHORT-TERM DEPARTMENTAL GOAL:

Review print, media, and electronic collections, adding and deleting titles as necessary and establishing on-line interlibrary loan services and other cooperative reciprocal access agreements with area agencies for resources not owned by the college.

MEASURABLE OBJECTIVE:

Systematically review holdings, acquiring and withdrawing titles, as appropriate, to develop a contemporary campus collection, participate in group access to OCLC interlibrary loan and in reciprocal access agreements.

DESCRIPTION OF ACTIVITIES:

LRC staff will continue to review book, media, and magazine collections, involving faculty in the review of holdings in their disciplines. Damaged and obsolete materials will be withdrawn. Contemporary titles supportive of the curricula will be acquired and processed into the collection. Through NEFLIN, LRC staff will continue on-line access to the OCLC interlibrary loan system expediting resource sharing. Other cooperative access agreements will be sought.
The Serials module of CCLA/LINCC will be implemented January 1997.

ANTICIPATED DATE FOR ACHIEVING OBJECTIVE: 1996-1997

RESOURCES NEEDED (facilities, training, involvement of other college departments, outside agency support, grant funding, etc.):

Assistance from other departments to review collections.
Computer support.

EVALUATION STRATEGY:

LRC collections will initially drop in quantity but improve in quality as current titles are added. ALA guidelines suggest minimums of 60,000 volumes, 500 magazine subscriptions, 750 video titles, and 8,000 other items. OCLC interlibrary loan access will continue. Direct access to other libraries will improve. Serials module will be implemented.

Revised 4/96

CENTRAL FLORIDA COMMUNITY COLLEGE
TACTICAL PLAN EVALUATION OF COMPONENT
for Academic Year 1996-1997

DIVISION
Division/Department:
Administrator:

INSTITUTIONAL GOAL:

DEPARTMENT OBJECTIVE:

DESCRIPTION OF ACTIVITIES:

PROPOSED COMPLETION DATE:

EVALUATION STRATEGY FOLLOWED: (Include a description of information gathered during evaluation.)

RESULTS OF EVALUATION:

A. ___ Objective fully met

B. ___ Objective partially met on or before proposed date

C. ___ Objective not met before proposed date

For "B" and "C", please indicate the reason below:

___ No funding received

___ Proposed deadline advanced

___ Partial progress, will readopt objective for next year

___ Objective to be modified for next year

Where is the evaluation information available for review? _____

7/96

Form 1

Unit - Level Institutional Effectiveness Program

Unit: Learning Resource Services

Date: September 23, 1997

Submitted by: W. Lee Hisle, AVP/LRS

I.   Statement of Unit Purpose

MISSION: Learning Resource Services will be a collaborative system of library information services, instructional technology, and instructional development whose aim is to support teaching and learning in Austin Community College by providing the excellent staff, resources, instruction and services needed by our community of users.

PRIMARY GOALS

Service

     Learning Resource Services will provide the highest quality service to all Austin Community College populations.

Resources

     Learning Resource Services will acquire, develop, and maintain the materials and equipment to meet the needs of the students, faculty and staff of Austin Community College.

Instruction/Learning

     Learning Resource Services will support Austin Community College's instructional mission. Learning Resource Services staff will educate users through the design and delivery of instruction to promote critical thinking and life-long learning.

SUPPORTING GOALS:

Access

     Learning Resource Services will provide equitable access to its resources instructional programs, and services for all Austin Community College populations.

Technology

     Learning Resource Services will investigate, acquire, utilize, maintain, and instruct in the use of traditional, as well as innovative and emerging technologies.

Facilities

     Learning Resource Services will acquire and maintain the facilities necessary to meet the needs of the students, faculty and staff of Austin Community College.

Management

     Learning Resource Services will be a learning organization that is open, collegial, well-organized, flexible, and responsive. Learning Resource Services will continually assess its services in response to the changing needs of its community for planning services and allocating resources.

Partnerships

     Learning Resource Services will maintain collaborative relationships within the College and with the larger community to be responsive to local, regional, and national needs, and initiatives and to make the most effective use of resources.

Distinction

     Learning Resource Services will be recognized, locally and nationally, for its program of services. Learning Resource Services has a commitment to improving the professions of its faculty and staff.

Form 2

II.   Assessment of Outcomes

Intended Outcomes	Assessment Procedures and Criteria
(Students):	
Students are aware of services provided by LRS Media Services, LRS Computer Centers, and LRS Library Services.	On the Student Satisfaction Survey questions dealing with student awareness, convenience, helpfulness, service, treatment, and the office overall, 75% of the respondents will rate LRS Media Services "3" or above.
Students find it convenient to get help from LRS Media Services, LRS Computer Centers, and LRS Library Services.	On the Student Satisfaction Survey questions dealing with student awareness, convenience, helpfulness, service, treatment, and the office overall, 75% of the respondents will rate LRS Computer Centers "3" or above.
Students find LRS Media Services, LRS Computer Centers, and LRS Library Services helpful in meeting their educational, personal, or career goals.	On the Student Satisfaction Survey questions dealing with student awareness, convenience, helpfulness, service, treatment, and the office overall, 75% of the respondents will rate LRS Library Services "3" or above.
Regarding LRS Media Services, LRS Computer Centers, and LRS Library Services, students are satisfied with services provided, treatment by staff, and the office overall.	

1997-98

Austin Community College

II.   Assessment of Outcomes

Intended Outcomes

Assessment Procedures and Criteria

(Employees):

Regarding LRS Media Services, LRS Computer Centers, and LRS Library Services, employees are satisfied with procedures for requesting support, with promptness of response, with quality of support, with service attitude, and with overall service.

On the Employee Satisfaction Survey questions dealing with procedures, promptness of service, quality of services, service attitude, and overall service, 75% of the respondents will rate LRS Media Services "3" or above.

On the Employee Satisfaction Survey questions dealing with procedures, promptness of service, quality of services, service attitude, and overall service, 75% of the respondents will rate LRS Computer Centers "3" or above.

On the Employee Satisfaction Survey questions dealing with procedures, promptness of service, quality of services, service attitude, and overall service, 75% of the respondents will rate LRS Library Services "3" or above.

1997-98

Macomb Community College
Program for Measuring Mission Effectiveness
Library

Mission Goal	Indicator	Measure	Timeline	Data Source	Benchmark	Results	Action Plan(s)
Academic Support Services: Library		9.G: Maintain or increase student knowlege of Library access	Each Semester	Quizzes Questionnaires Library Material Utilization Report	95% of students randomly tested in five classes will demonstrate library access competence	1996-97:	
Academic Support Services: Library		10.F: Maintain or increase library user satisfaction with library services	Annually	ABC Survey Library Users Survey	82%	1991-92	
Academic Support Services: Library		12.G: Maintain or increase the number of library users utilizing DALNET Databases	Quarterly	DALNET Databases Utilization Report	5% Increase over last quarter	1995-96:	
Academic Support Services: All Units		14.C: All academic support services will be reviewed at least once over a three-year period	Annually on a rotating 3-year basis	SS Review Report	100% of support services scheduled	1996-97:	Develop the Academic Support Services Review Process and Instrument

A:MEASMIS.EFF

Macomb Community College
Program for Measuring Mission Effectiveness
Library

Mission Goal	Indicator	Measure	Timeline	Data Source	Benchmark	Results	Action Plan(s)
Academic Support Services		14.D: Maintain or increase the number of MCC employees participating in professional development activities as determined through MCC priorities	Annually	EIS enrollment data (as kept by Registration area, pertaining to staff development provided by Cont. Ed. Dept.) Internal CES Unit Records	1993-94: 4 unit meetings/yr	1994-95: 1994-95:	
Advanced Education							
Career Education							
Community Development							
Community Education and Personal Enrichment Programs							
Customized Education							
General Studies Education							
Transfer Education							
Academic Support Services: Library		14.G: Maintain or increase the relevance and availability of library resources	Annually	Inventory Surveys Focus Groups	60%	1994-95:	

TRANSITION TO THE FUTURE
LRS STRATEGIC PLAN 1998-2002

LRS MISSION

Learning Resource Services will be a collaborative system of library information services, instructional technology, and instructional development whose aim is to support teaching and learning at Austin Community College by providing the excellent staff, resources, instruction and services needed by our community of users.

Learning Resource Services
Austin Community College
Austin, Texas
18 August 1997

Austin Community College

LEARNING RESOURCE SERVICES

CONTENTS

LRS STRATEGIC PLANNING GROUP

W. Lee Hisle, Ph.D.
Associate Vice President, LRS

Toma Iglehart, MLS
Reference Librarian, RGC

Richard L. Smith, Ph.D.
Manager, Instructional Technology and Development

Margaret Peloquin, MLIS
Head Librarian, RVS

LEARNING RESOURCE SERVICES

INTRODUCTION

Learning Resource Services (LRS) has provided quality information and instructional technology support services to the ACC community for many years. The *LRS Strategic Plan 1992-97* has helped guide the growth of the department and helped us to understand how we could be more effective.

A new strategic planning process was begun some 18 months ago. It has involved dozens of LRS faculty, professional and classified staff members, as well as other ACC faculty, staff and students. The planning process facilitated an understanding of the directions LRS should be moving in order to continue effective support of the ACC educational mission.

Transition to the Future: The LRS Strategic Plan 1998-2002 will guide the development of programs and services over the next five years. It will link LRS evaluation efforts with annual goals and objectives, and it will link goals and objectives to budget requests and priorities. Finally, some 4 years from now, this plan will link LRS to the next strategic planning process.

The LRS consists of three internal departments of Library Services, Instructional Technology and Development, and Technical Services and Automation. Learning Resource Centers are the physical locations in which these departments offer services to the ACC community. LRS provides support for effective teaching and learning, both within a classrooms (including virtual classrooms), within Learning Resource Centers and from remote locations.

My thanks to all those in LRS and in ACC who helped bring this document into being. From your efforts, the LRS program is stronger and more capable of supporting the college's instructional needs.

W. Lee Hisle, Ph.D.
Associate Vice-President
Learning Resource Services

LEARNING RESOURCE SERVICES

OVERVIEW OF THE ORGANIZATION

Overview of LRS Organization

Learning Resource Services is an integrated system of instructional support services consisting of three internal departments: Library Services, Instructional Technology and Development, and Technical Services and Automation. Learning Resource Centers are the physical locations in which services are delivered. LRS is organized as a centralized, district-wide operation under the leadership of the Associate Vice-President for LRS. The Associate Vice-President reports directly to the Executive Vice-President.

Although LRS is a centralized, district-wide organization, conscious effort is made to ensure relevance and participation at the local, campus level. Members of LRS staff serve on campus committees and participate in campus leadership activities. Special collections are maintained for campuses depending on unique academic offerings. Each campus holds meetings of all LRS professional staff to foster cooperation among the LRS departments on that campus.

LRS is managed using a matrix-model of participatory management. Line authority comes from the Associate Vice-President and the Management Team which consists of the five Head Librarians and the Manager of Instructional Technology and Development. Functional work areas of LRS are managed by committee-teams of faculty, professional and classified staff members. Committees exist to manage, for example, the Library Automation System, Staff Development, LRS Instruction, Collection Development, and Public Relations. These committees are chaired by regular LRS faculty and staff, as well as by Management Team members. The committees report to the Associate Vice-President who consults with the Management Team on operational and policy issues. The Associate Vice-President also maintains an ad-hoc LRS Focus Group, made up of LRS faculty and staff, to deal with operational issues and insure communication from the bottom-up.

Since 1992, LRS has operated under the guidance of the *LRS Strategic Plan, 1992-97*. All employee and program evaluations, annual goals and objectives, and budget development efforts are linked to the LRS Strategic Plan. Development of the new plan, *Transition to the Future: LRS Strategic Plan, 1998-2002*, was started some 18 months ago.

Approximately 100 ACC employees work in Learning Resource Services at the eleven campuses or sites where LRCs are operated. LRS circulated over 300,000 materials in FY97, accommodated nearly one million visits by ACC faculty, staff, and students; and answered over 170,000 reference questions. In addition, some 12,000 students participated in one the LRS instructional programs. The materials collection consists of nearly 120,000 volumes.

Performance Goals are set for committees, as well as for faculty and staff, each academic year. Evaluation is based on goal achievement. Committee Conveners are evaluated by their peers; they in turn evaluate their committee members. That information is transmitted to line supervisors to be used in individual performance reviews.

Reorganization of Learning Resources as a district-wide centralized operation since 1985 has benefitted the college community of students, faculty and staff in many ways. In general, the centralized organization has increased accountability for LRS operations. Other benefits include:

- quality of services is consistent in all LRCs in the district
- policies and procedures are consistent across the district
- resource sharing between campuses is easily accomplished since collection development funds are centralized
- the automation system serves all ACC users equally; cataloging standards are consistent in the district
- library instructional efforts can be developed and implemented college-wide
- technology planning for LRS is done district-wide, maximizing the useful life of equipment
- district-wide acquisition of materials and supplies brings cost savings
- faculty and staff can be assigned to LRS committees based on their expertise rather than to satisfy geographical requirements
- staff development is planned for district-wide participation leading to better overall service to students and faculty

LRS has a commitment to improve its operations and quality of service through continual examination of its organizational structure, and a willingness to make improvements as appropriate.

LEARNING RESOURCE SERVICES

VISION FOR THE FUTURE

In perhaps the greatest revolution in education since the advent of the printing press over 500 years ago, the electronic information age is changing the way learning and teaching take place whether in a classroom, a laboratory, at home, at work, or in a learning resource center. The microchip pervades our personal and professional lives and, increasingly, all aspects of education will change as a result. Yet, the time-tested, traditional approaches to education and research retain value and relevance. Respecting the past, understanding the present, and anticipating the future, LRS strives to provide the information and instructional support services needed at ACC.

All Learning Resource Services are directed toward the achievement of our mission, goals, and strategic objectives while supporting the mission of the college. Support for teaching and learning, whether accomplished in the classroom, via distance learning methods, or via independent effort in Learning Resource Centers, will be the focus of our energies.

The LRS will provide essential library, instructional technology, and instructional development services in an integrated system of support to the educational programs, instructional goals, and student needs at ACC. These services will use whatever methods are most appropriate to the audience, from traditional to the most innovative. Our efforts will match pedagogy with appropriate methods of support.

Instruction / Learning

The Electronic Information Age is producing an enormous amount of data; students, faculty and staff are bombarded with messages from newspapers, television, radio, movies, video, magazines, and lately, electronic sources such as CD-ROMs and the Internet. They may spend an inordinate amount of time processing these messages, but not necessarily becoming more informed.

Information literacy skills (critical-thinking, life-long learning, and effective use of electronic information) underlies the LRS instructional program. The LRS instruction program will educate students on the research process and use of information resources for class completion, life-long learning and recreation. At the same time, it will satisfy those immediate needs within a value system of providing information literacy skills. LRS professionals will be actively involved in curriculum development to advance information literacy in ACC students.

Instructional programming to teach effective use of electronic resources, for research and classroom improvement, will be developed and offered to students, faculty and staff. This instruction will be delivered as credit courses or non-credit workshops for small and large groups, as well as one-on-one.

LRS will specifically target services to improve classroom performance by ACC faculty through Instructional Development Centers. Possible services will include individual consultations with faculty, provision of teaching labs for self-analysis, instructional short courses and online tutorials. Services will be linked to faculty evaluations and other aspects of the ACC Faculty Development Program. Instructional development for traditional and electronic modes of instruction will be provided.

Resources

Materials collections (print, AV, computer software, etc.) in support of the ACC curriculum will be expanded and will include online, full-image periodicals, newspapers and reference sources. These materials will be acquired and maintained in the most expeditious, cost-advantageous, technologically appropriate method possible. Partnerships between classroom faculty, librarians, and ITD professionals will be used to ensure collection development which reflects the needs of the ACC community.

Professionals will serve as bibliographers of Internet resources, as they do of traditional print and audiovisual materials, linking faculty and students to resources relevant to their area of study. Electronic reserves will be implemented to serve students regardless of the location of a reserve material or the location of the student. Document delivery services will take advantage of new technology to speed access to materials across the district. Many LRS electronic resources will be available across the network to faculty in their offices or students at home.

Access

The idea of community in America is changing as society moves from a public to a private orientation, heralded by home-theater and electronic Internet villages with chat rooms. Education programs must accommodate the changing information needs of this new type of society. LRS will continue to provide all the traditional library services, however we will also provide expanded access to new, electronic information sources. Because these digital resources are disseminated through the Internet, access can potentially be extended to all ACC LRCs, classrooms, labs, and offices. In addition, resources will be available from home. To serve working students, extended hours in LRCs will be provided in the district.

An integrated LRS automation system will be available that offers access, through one search engine, to multiple electronic sources, as well as electronic reserves, patron-initiated interlibrary loan, and access to shared electronic resource systems.

LRS will support Open-Campus students with special, directed services (which may include 2-way video reference, document delivery, 800-numbers, etc.) and access to electronic resources from distant sites or from home.

Technology

LRS will maintain open computer labs for student and faculty access to productivity and information tools. These spaces will serve as small and large group teaching facilities for the LRS instructional program as well.

Equipment will be current and sufficiently deployed to satisfy the educational needs of students and faculty, as well as the workplace needs of LRS staff. Robust PC workstations loaded with productivity and information software will be available throughout the LRCs. The LRS Technology Plan will be continually updated and will guide technology acquisition and use in the LRS.

Instructional development will increase in importance as faculty and students integrate electronic educational tools and methods into classroom experiences. Instructors will use Web pages as classroom aides and students will turn in assignments using digital media. Instructional development will use teams of information professionals and classroom faculty to develop programming.

Facilities

The blurring of boundaries among traditional LRS areas, e.g., computer centers, library reference, etc., will lead LRS to incorporate an Information Commons concept (open-access computing and media-viewing facilities) in its Learning Resource Centers. The Information Commons will serve general students, special-needs students, and CIS students. Integration of services in LRCs will provide students with greater access to information and computer resources, as well as providing the college with better space utilization.

Electronic classrooms will be available at every campus to enable innovative use of networked resources in instruction.

Staff

Staff who are technologically-adept, have a cooperative attitude, excellent public service orientation, and who can facilitate the use of instructional and information technology will be employed, developed, and retained. Staff will be cross-trained to function effectively in an information-diverse environment. Staff will be selected with the personal qualities necessary to interact effectively with a community college clientele. Sufficient permanent staff will be employed to serve the needs of LRS clients and the ACC community reducing LRS dependence on hourly employees.

Management

LRS will be an integrated system of instructional and information technology programs and services. It will operate with a district-wide perspective to maximize resource sharing, to provide consistency of services, central accountability, and to achieve a unified mission. LRS managers will model a high standard of service-orientation, work ethic, and commitment to the ACC mission.

The management of LRS will be flexible, without compromising quality, in adapting to changes at ACC, advances in technology, and in meeting LRS users' expectations and needs. Electronic communications for meetings, internal documents, policies and procedures, minutes, LRS publications, and collection development routines will be used.

Partnerships

Classroom faculty will see the LRS program as a partner in achieving student excellence through teaching and learning. LRS will partner with Student Services to meet the information needs of at-risk and special needs student populations.

Local cooperative agreements (with libraries, businesses, etc.) will be expanded and strengthened as necessary to improve service to our faculty and students. The LRS will participate fully in state-wide initiatives for resource sharing.

Distinction and Standards

LRS will emphasize quality in all services which will result in state and national recognition for its programs and operations. LRS will guide and measure progress by the use of applicable professional standards, benchmarks, and by internal and external evaluations.

LEARNING RESOURCE SERVICES

MISSION AND GOALS -- 1998-2002

MISSION: Learning Resource Services will be a collaborative system of library information services, instructional technology, and instructional development whose aim is to support teaching and learning at Austin Community College by providing the excellent staff, resources, instruction and services needed by our community of users.

PRIMARY GOALS:

Service

Learning Resource Services will provide the highest quality service to all Austin Community College populations.

Resources

Learning Resource Services will acquire, develop, and maintain the materials and equipment to meet the needs of the students, faculty and staff of Austin Community College.

Instruction / Learning

Learning Resource Services will support Austin Community College's instructional mission. Learning Resource Services staff will educate users through the design and delivery of instruction to promote critical thinking and life-long learning.

SUPPORTING GOALS:

Access

Learning Resource Services will provide equitable access to its resources, instructional programs, and services for all Austin Community College populations.

Technology

Learning Resource Services will investigate, acquire, utilize, maintain, and instruct in the use of traditional, as well as innovative and emerging technologies.

Staff

Learning Resource Services will attract and retain staff who are knowledgeable, motivated, adaptable, service-oriented, and effective. Learning Resource Services has a commitment to provide continuing education and training for its staff.

Facilities

Learning Resource Services will acquire and maintain the facilities necessary to meet the needs of the students, faculty and staff of Austin Community College.

Management

Learning Resource Services will be a learning organization that is open, collegial, well-organized, flexible, and responsive. Learning Resource Services will continually assess its services in response to the changing needs of its community for planning services and allocating resources.

Partnerships

Learning Resource Services will maintain collaborative relationships within the College and with the larger community to be responsive to local, regional, and national needs and initiatives, and to make the most effective use of resources.

Distinction

Learning Resource Services will be recognized, locally and nationally, for its program of services. Learning Resource Services has a commitment to improving the professions of its faculty and staff.

Standards

Learning Resource Services will endeavor to meet the accepted standards and principles of its professions.

LEARNING RESOURCE SERVICES

STRATEGIC OBJECTIVES 1998

OBJ 1   Build a materials collection which better meets the current and future needs of the ACC community.   [Goal: Resources, Access, Technology, Standards]

TASK 001   Provide needed funds to maintain the materials collections (print, media, software, electronic resources, etc.) using a standard formula of replacing 5% of the materials per year.

TASK 002   Provide funds needed to begin to phase in expansion of the collection to improve the ratio of students to material based on ACRL standards.

TASK 003   Analyze current collections against ACC curricular requirements and anticipated needs.

TASK 004   Analyze current collections deficiencies at smaller campuses and investigate ways to expand student access to materials.

TASK 005   Analyze current collections by comparing the collections to national standards.

OBJ 2   Increase student access to resources.   [Goal: Access, Service, Resources, Technology, Partnerships]

TASK 006   Acquire and install the upgrade or replacement of the Dynix library automation system.

TASK 007   Provide networked electronic resources to the ACC communities.

OBJ 3   Study current LRS space utilization in the College and implement viable changes.   [Goal: Facilities, Technology, Partnerships, Service, Resources, Staff, Instruction/Learning]

TASK 008   Provide expandible and flexible LRC facilities and operations -- suitable collection, services, and new staff -- at the new Central East Austin Campus.

TASK 009   Provide multi-disciplinary electronic classrooms at CYP, NRG, PIN, RVS, and Central East Austin campuses for general campus use.

TASK 010   Create a multi-purpose area in the RGC media viewing area with computers so that students can have access to IT help and electronic resources.

TASK 011   Investigate redesigning LRC spaces integrating electronic information sources and services into traditional space.

OBJ 4   Provide staff for adequate service at all existing and planned LRS locations.   [Goal: Staff, Service, Management, Standards, Access]

TASK 012   Fund appropriate staffing levels at all LRCs.

TASK 013   Restore and increase hourly funds to support basic services.

OBJ 5   Support the instructional efforts of the ACC faculty.   [Goal: Instruction/Learning, Staff, Access, Technology]

TASK 014 Add an Instructional Development Specialist at the PIN campus to serve PIN faculty and DSL program.

OBJ 6   Collaborate with other ACC groups to best plan for and utilize technological resources at ACC.   [Goal: Partnerships, Technology, Resources, Management]

TASK 015 Maintain the LRS Technology Replacement Plan in light of the College's plan and provide funds to implement needed changes.

TASK 016 Provide funds to implement the LRS Technology Replacement Plan to include the replacement of aging instructional audiovisual equipment.

OBJ 7   Provide more staff development and training opportunities.   [Goal: Staff, Management]

TASK 017 Provide funding for additional staff attendance at workshops and training sessions.

TASK 018 Offer in-house training through the LRS Staff Development Committee on issues identified by staff.

TASK 019 Provide funding for classified staff training and development.

OBJ 8   Foster open and informative communications among LRS staff.   [Goal: Staff, Management]

TASK 020 Have at least two all-LRS meetings per academic year.

TASK 021 Have at least 3 meetings of all LRS professional staff per academic year.

TASK 022 Promote the use of ACCnet to facilitate communications within LRS.

TASK 023 Continue to improve and implement the LRS decision-making structure.

OBJ 9   Develop a plan to better standardize LRS services and procedures across the district.   [Goal: Management, Service, Standards, Access]

TASK 024 Identify areas for standardization of LRS services and procedures.

TASK 025 Assign teams to address specific standardization issues and propose changes.

OBJ 10   Strengthen LRS operations through exemplary leadership and management. [Goal: Management, Service]

TASK 026 Provide a clear, consistent vision and direction.

TASK 027 Continue to develop the team concept for optimal operations.

OBJ 11   Expand resource sharing, particularly of electronic resources, with other institutions.   [Goal: Partnerships, Resources, Technology, Access]

TASK 028 Investigate new models of resource sharing with local or regional institutions.

OBJ 12   Use technological advances to provide options for better serving ACC communities.   [Goal: Technology, Service, Access]

T<small>ASK</small> 029   Provide reference service through the LRS Web site.

OBJ 13   Offer innovative LRS instruction.   [Goal: Instruction/Learning, Technology, Distinction]

T<small>ASK</small> 030   Utilize electronic classrooms for training and workshops.

T<small>ASK</small> 031   Implement a "for-credit" course in information access and electronic resources.

T<small>ASK</small> 032   Continue to improve the course on information access and electronic resources offered through CCBD.

T<small>ASK</small> 033   Analyze current program of LRS instruction and develop alternative programs if needed.

OBJ 14   Gain recognition of LRS as a program of distinction.   [Goal: Distinction, Staff]

T<small>ASK</small> 034   Encourage LRS staff to participate in professional organizations.

T<small>ASK</small> 035   Encourage LRS staff to contribute to the improvement of their professions through publications and presentations of papers and workshops.

LEARNING RESOURCE SERVICES

STRATEGIC OBJECTIVES 1999-2002

OBJ 1   Expand LRS services for users employing electronic access to information resources.   [Goal: Service, Resources, Technology]

OBJ 2   Develop and implement outcomes-based evaluation system for LRS services. [Goal: Service, Management, Standards]

OBJ 3   Develop and maintain public services orientation in all LRS staff. [Goal: Service, Staff]

OBJ 4   Explore new models to integrate LRS services and implement as appropriate. [Goal: Service, Management]

OBJ 5   Evaluate existing LRS resources (collections, equipment, etc.) and review utilization to facilitate resource development and management. [Goal: Resources, Management, Standards]

OBJ 6   Maintain adequate funds to support existing and new resources as enrollments grow and programs change.   [Goal: Resources, Management, Standards]

OBJ 7   Integrate LRS instruction into more classes.   [Goal: Instruction / Learning]

OBJ 8   Continue to evaluate and improve the way LRS delivers instruction.   [Goal: Instruction / Learning, Management]

OBJ 9   Expand LRS instructional offerings to the ACC community, especially in light of emerging electronic resources and technology. [Goal: Instruction / Learning, Technology]

OBJ 10   Support the improvement of faculty teaching effectiveness. [Goal: Instruction / Learning, Partnerships]

OBJ 11   Provide increased hours of access to LRS resources and facilities. [Goal: Access, Resources, Facilities]

OBJ 12   Provide remote access to the LRS catalog and other electronic resources for the ACC community.   [Goal: Access, Resources, Technology]

OBJ 13   Improve student access to classroom reserve materials and periodical articles.   [Goal: Access, Resources]

OBJ 14   Increase student access to electronic resources in the the LRCs. [Goal: Access, Resources, Technology, Facilities]

OBJ 15   Investigate and implement technological innovations which will improve LRS support of instruction and learning.   [Goal: Technology, Instruction / Learning]

OBJ 16   Investigate and disseminate information about emerging technologies to the college.   [Goal: Technology, Partnerships]

OBJ 17   Maintain adequate funds to acquire new and replacement hardware and software. [Goal: Technology, Management]

OBJ 18   Use electronic technology to improve communications and management. [Goal: Technology, Management]

OBJ 19   Continue to revise the LRS Technology Plan to meet the changing College environment.   [Goal: Technology, Management]

OBJ 20   Seek to obtain compensation for staff commensurate with their job responsibilities. [Goal: Staff, Management]

OBJ 21   Emphasize LRS staff development and training.   [Goal: Staff, Standards, Distinction]

OBJ 22   Explore alternative compensation and reward systems for exemplary job performance by LRS staff. [Goal: Staff, Management]

OBJ 23   Obtain additional staff to meet changing service demands and increased use of information technology. [Goal: Staff, Management, Technology]

OBJ 24   Investigate existing LRS space and reorganize to achieve best use. [Goal: Facilities, Service]

OBJ 25   Seek to expand LRS space.   [Goal: Facilities, Management]

OBJ 26   Provide LRS input into planning new ACC facilities.   [Goal: Facilities, Management, Partnerships]

OBJ 27   Provide a quality study, research, and development environment for students and faculty, as well as quality work environment for staff. [Goal: Facilities, Service, Staff]

OBJ 28   Maintain awareness of technological advances that have an impact on LRS activities and implement those appropriate to LRS operations.   [Goal: Management, Technology]

OBJ 29   Improve methods of communications with the ACC community to identify needed services and to promote existing services.   [Goal: Management, Service]

OBJ 30   Evaluate and revise the LRS organizational structure as the College's changing environment warrants. [Goal: Management, Standards]

OBJ 31   Increase among LRS staff understanding of LRS operations, organizational structure and the individual's role in a service organization.   [Goal: Management, Staff, Service]

OBJ 32   Evaluate LRS operations and services and implement strategies for improvement as appropriate.   [Goal: Management, Standards]

OBJ 33   Continue to develop relationships with academic areas to improve teaching and learning.   [Goal: Partnerships, Instruction / Learning]

OBJ 34   Continue to work with all College departments to improve service to the ACC community.   [Goal: Partnerships, Service]

OBJ 35   Develop beneficial relationships with local or regional libraries and educational entities.   [Goal: Partnerships, Management]

OBJ 36   Present and promote LRS programs and staff internally and outside the ACC environment.   [Goal: Distinction, Management, Service, Staff]

OBJ 37   Promote participation in professional organizations, activities, research, publication, meetings, and committees.   [Goal: Distinction, Staff]

OBJ 38   Continue to evaluate LRS programs and actions in light of accepted professional standards and principles.   [Goal: Standards, Management]

LEARNING RESOURCE SERVICES

EVALUATION AND ASSESSMENT

EVALUATION OF ANNUAL PROGRESS

LRS formally evaluates progress toward achieving its Mission, Goals and Objectives each year. Tasks are set by individuals, committees, and the LRS Management Team which define what is to be done each year to satisfy the Strategic Objectives. An annual review of accomplishments is done at the start of the academic year to measure progress.

ORGANIZATIONAL PROGRESS

Annual reports, which detail objectives and tasks for the coming year and accomplishments for the past year, are required of all LRS committees and organizational units. Objectives and accomplishments are tied specifically to the goals of the LRS Strategic Plan. The Associate Vice-President meets periodically throughout the year with committee conveners to assess performance.

Statistics of LRS activity for the previous fiscal year are collected in the fall. These figures are used for completion of local, state, and national data collection efforts as well as for comparison of ACC performance to that of other colleges.

Every fall, the *LRS Annual Report* is published which summarizes the accomplishments and plans for the department along with appropriate statistical measures of performance.

INDIVIDUAL PROGRESS

LRS engages in semi-annual evaluation of professional performance and annual evaluation of classified staff. At the beginning of the academic year, professionals propose their personal objectives for the year, linked to specific LRS Goals and Strategic Objectives which are reviewed and approved by supervisors. This review includes professional growth activities. At the mid-year review, these personal objectives are reviewed to ascertain progress and needed adjustment. The ACC evaluation summary is completed at this time as well.

OUTCOMES ASSESSMENT

As mandated by the Southern Association of Colleges and Schools, LRS participates in annual assessment of its effectiveness in coordination with College efforts. A mechanism for conducting this assessment will be devised in conjunction with the Office of Institutional Effectiveness which satisfies the requirements of SACS and the needs of LRS and the College.

STRATEGIC PLAN REVIEW

We anticipate a formal review and revision of the LRS Strategic Plan in five years. The process to reevaluate the plan will begin in the spring of 2001 with a revision projected for the summer of 2002.

LRS STRATEGIC PLAN 1998-2002
APPENDICES

LEARNING RESOURCE SERVICES

AUSTIN COMMUNITY COLLEGE — MISSION AND PURPOSE

Austin Community College will be a learning organization, one that engages in self-evaluation, self-renewal, and self-sustaining growth. We pledge to assess and understand the needs of our communities and to deliver educational programs and services that meet those needs in the most effective manner.

Austin Community College operates on the belief that open access to quality post-secondary educational experiences is vital in a rapidly changing democratic society. Therefore, the College exists to provide such educational opportunities to all the people of the Austin, Texas, area. Hence, Austin Community College maintains an "open door" admissions policy, offers a comprehensive variety of post-secondary educational programs, and actively seeks to eliminate barriers in the educational process. The legal purpose of the Austin Community College is prescribed by the Texas Legislature:

1. Technical programs up to two years in length leading to associate degrees or certificates;
2. Vocational programs leading directly to employment in semiskilled and skilled occupations;
3. Freshman and sophomore courses in arts and sciences;
4. Continuing adult education for occupational or cultural upgrading;
5. Compensatory educational programs designed to fulfill the commitment of an admissions policy allowing the enrollment of disadvantaged students;
6. A continuing program of counseling and guidance designed to assist students in achieving their individual educational goals;
7. Workforce development programs designed to meet local and statewide needs;
8. Adult literacy and other basic skills programs for adults; and
9. Such other purposes as may be prescribed by the Texas Higher Education Coordinating Board, or local governing boards in the best interest of post-secondary education in Texas.

Austin Community College offers the following types of programs, services, and instruction to fulfill its purpose and to satisfy state law for public junior and community colleges:

1. Student-centered instruction that seeks to aid students in their educational endeavors while demanding quality performance.
2. Vocational and technical programs of varying lengths leading to certificates or degrees.
3. Freshman and sophomore-level academic courses leading to an associate degree or serving as the base of a baccalaureate degree program at a four-year institution.
4. Continuing adult education for academic, occupational, professional, and cultural enhancement.
5. Special instructional programs and tutorial services to assist under-prepared students and others who wish special assistance to achieve their educational goals.
6. A continuing program of counseling and advising designed to assist students in achieving their individual educational and occupational goals.
7. A program of library, media, and testing services to support instruction.
8. Contracted instructional programs and services for area employers that promote economic development.

LEARNING RESOURCE SERVICES

SURVEY AND FOCUS GROUP RESULTS

SURVEY OF LRS SERVICES

LRS conducted surveys during the spring of 1996 to determine whether our client base was satisfied with our services. There were three separate surveys:

Faculty Survey
Distributed to all full-time faculty and part-time faculty

Student Survey
Distributed to a random sample of students in the classroom

Customer Survey
Distributed within the Learning Resource Centers

The results of the surveys were analyzed by the Strategic Planning Group and the LRS Management Team and used in strategic planning.

ACC EFFECTIVENESS SURVEYS

During the late fall, the ACC Office of Institutional Effectiveness conducted a survey of students and ACC employees to determine the effectiveness of ACC support services. LRS was one of the support services surveyed. Results from the surveys were analyzed by the LRS Management Team and incorporated into strategic planning.

FOCUS GROUPS

In April 1997, two focus groups were organized — a student group and a group consisting of ACC faculty and staff — for the purpose of providing information pertinent to LRS strategic planning and for review of our draft mission and goals.

The LRS Strategic Planning Group met with each focus group on the afternoon of 18 April 1997.

FACULTY/STAFF FOCUS GROUP

At a request from Frank Friedman, Executive Vice President of Academic and Student Affairs, a group of faculty and staff were invited to participate in a review of LRS efforts and to help ensure that the new plan meet the needs of ACC faculty and staff.

LRS Strategic Plan -- APPENDIX B

The group accepted the mission and goals in principle and offered comments and suggestions as to LRS services. In general, LRS services were viewed very favorably. Suggestions for formal library research classes, library orientation, making the LRC a friendlier place, more publicity about LRS services to special populations, and more open access were made.

The group agreed that having future meetings of a faculty/staff focus group would benefit both LRS and the faculty and staff.

STUDENT FOCUS GROUP

In cooperation with the ACC Student Activities Office, a group of students were invited to participate in a focus group to review the proposed mission and goals and to suggest ways in which students might be better served by LRS.

The students offered a number of suggestions including services to special populations, consistency in service and hours, more open hours to accommodate students who cannot go to the LRCs during traditional hours, more orientation and workshops about LRS services and resources, and better publicity about what is available in the LRCs.

LEARNING RESOURCE SERVICES

LRS TECHNOLOGY PLAN — SUMMARY

The LRS Technology Plan was developed by the LRS Technology-Networking-Web Committee during the Spring, 1997 semester. The Plan includes information on seven areas within LRS where technology has an impact. The areas include:

1. LRS Automation
2. Office/Work Activities
3. Instructional Development and Production
4. Public Access Technology
5. Training and Electronic Classrooms
6. Instructional/Classroom Support
7. Duplication and Document Imaging

For each area, the Technology Plan includes the following information.

◆ Current State -- a general statement of services, activities and resources available in FY97. Resources includes a complete inventory of computer and media hardware and computer software.

◆ Future Direction -- a general statement of how technology might be used in each of the seven areas in FY98 and following years. This subsection also discusses the impact technology will have on ACC students and faculty, as well as on LRS's needs for hardware, software, facilities, staff and training. Budget implications for each area are also provided.

Area Highlights

1. LRS Automation

The LRS automation system is a college-wide system which provides external and internal support to students, faculty and staff. The system includes an on-line Patron Access Catalog, and modules for managing circulation, acquisitions, cataloging and serials control. The system is available at all ACC sites either via INet or dial-up .

LRS plans a major upgrade for FY98 to replace the existing Dynix library automation system. The new hardware will provide expanded port capacity for existing and expanded sites such as Central East Austin, for access by students from home, and for expanded access by faculty and staff from offices via the ACCNet intranet. Replacement of terminals with PC workstations will permit graphical or Web-based user interfaces for patrons and staff, as well as expanded software capabilities for connection to on-line resources and the Internet.

LRS Strategic Plan -- APPENDIX C

2. Office/Work Activities

LRS plans to replace all LRS personal computer workstations and terminals with ACCNet compatible, multi-use workstations. This will allow all LRS staff to access internet and ACCNet intranet resources. Other goals include standardizing office productivity software, establishing procedures for intranet-based record keeping and information sharing, and providing printer sharing for office computers.

3. Instructional Development and Production

The majority of technology-based instructional development and production activities are performed by the LRS Department of Instructional Technology and Development (ITD) and in the LRS Media Centers. The LRS also provides Faculty Productivity Centers within LRS Computer Centers so that faculty may do some of their own production work.

LRS will continue to provide the majority of these services, with an increasing focus on using ACCNet and the Web for support services and as an instructional resource. LRS will provide Web access to its electronic catalog, CD-ROM databases and on-line resources, as well as offer on-line services such as equipment reservations, reserves, reference services and on-line training. LRS will upgrade the Faculty Productivity Centers into Instructional Development Centers in FY98, with expanded services and production capabilities. LRS will update production hardware and services to meet the changing technology needs of the College.

4. Public Access Technology

Public access technology is available to students, staff and faculty through LRS Computer Centers, Media Centers, Faculty Productivity Centers, Reference and CD-ROM workstations, and an on-line CD-ROM LAN.

LRS will move toward an *Information Commons* model for open-access computing and resource sharing. This model increases reliance on multi-purpose PC-based workstations which provide networked access to local and remote information resources, as well as instructional and productivity software. This model is used in the Central East Austin LRS facilities plan. The LRS also plans to network all Computer Centers using Windows NT, to expand the CD-ROM LAN, restructure media viewing areas, and establish networked printing services.

5. Training and Electronic Classrooms

LRS offers training to ACC faculty and staff in the production and use of instructional technologies, and to students in the use of information technologies. Training is provided in a variety of formats (one-on-one, small group, large group) for a variety of topics (Web page design, using electronic resources, etc.). Training is offered in Faculty Productivity Centers, Computer Centers, other ACC computing facilities (labs and electronic classrooms), and on individual computers located throughout the LRCs.

LRS will continue to develop and deliver training which meets the instructional and information needs of faculty, staff and students. LRS will expand face-to-face training opportunities, provide additional on-line, self-directed training activities and will publicize all training activities through print and Web-based announcements. LRS will promote the need for additional interdisciplinary electronic classrooms college-wide.

6. Instructional/Classroom Support

LRS supports classroom instruction not only through development activities, but also by providing media equipment and a collection of commercially produced instructional materials.

LRS plans to expand classroom support by providing additional multi-media carts and classroom mounted televisions and VCRs. The LRS non-print collection will also be expanded. LRS plans to implement an AV Replacement Plan, similar in scope to the ACC computer replacement plan. Such a plan will ensure that aging technologies are replaced on a consistent schedule.

7. Duplication

Duplication in LRS is a multi-faceted activity. LRS provides faculty, staff and students with facilities for photo duplication, microform duplication, audiotape duplication and image scanning. Video duplication is provided by LRS staff on a limited basis.

Duplication services in LRS will change as patrons gain access to networked full-text resources, as reserves are provided in electronic form, and as document imaging becomes more common. LRS will implement solutions to these problems as they arise.

The LRS Technology Plan is a document in progress. The success of any technology plan is dependent on a number of factors, including the instructional needs of the institution, the swiftness of technological change, and the budget available to implement change. The LRS Technology Plan was used for FY98 strategic planning both in LRS and for the College's Technology Plan. The current LRS Technology Plan will be reviewed and revised yearly, to see that LRS is meeting the instructional needs of the College. The complete Plan will be available at the LRS web site.

LEARNING RESOURCE SERVICES

LRS STATISTICS — SUMMARY

	1992-1993	1993-1994	1994-1995	1995-1996	% change 1995-1996	4 year % change
Door Count	769,896	801,091	845,915	886,067	4.75%	15.09%
Materials/ Circulations - All formats	285,000	231,443	292,770	316,227	8.01%	10.96%
Volumes (all formats)	109,724	114,124	115,672	123,063	6.39%	12.16%
Titles (all formats)	64,298	67,108	66,458	71,215	7.16%	10.76%
Books						
Total volumes	97,523	101,622	102,926	109,847	6.72%	12.64%
Total titles	58,297	60,648	60,067	64,666	7.66%	10.93%
Audiovisual (total titles)	5,378	5,456	5,386	5,473	1.62%	1.77%
Computer Software (total titles)	623	1,004	1,005	1,076	7.06%	72.71%
Microforms (unduplicated)	190	179	179	186	3.91%	-2.11%
Subscriptions (duplicated)	1,458	2,211	2,194	2,205	0.50%	51.23%
Reference Transactions*	131,252	151,447	162,867	85,326	-47.61%	-34.99%
Library Instruction						
Students in Formal LUI Programs	8,565	11,703	11,880	12,122	2.04%	41.53%
Students in English Composition I	6,453	8,500	6,075	6,750	11.11%	4.60%
Classroom Presentations	159	164	251	270	7.57%	69.81%
Students at Presentations			4465	6592	47.64%	n/a
LUI Reference Questions	8,900	6,242	6,396	6,594	3.10%	-25.91%
Fee/Fine Collections	$48,906	$48,821	$56,317	$54,944	-2.44%	12.35%
Online Searches	155	133	81	278	243.21%	79.35%
Interlibrary Loans						
Lender	226	n/a	44	197	347.73%	-12.83%
Borrower	372	706	371	262	-29.38%	-29.57%
Headcount	109,628	153,491	109,254	148,021	35.48%	35.02%
Equipment Circulation	9,941	11,440	10,913	11,558	5.91%	16.27%
Program Circulation	3,314	8,729	3,677	2,938	-20.10%	-11.35%
Production						
Graphics (computer)	5,356	7,016	7,410	7,759	4.71%	44.87%
Photography	1,455	2,981	925	290	-68.65%	-80.07%
Television	224	206	240	381	58.75%	70.09%
Audio	1,089	505	970	336	-65.36%	-69.15%
Equipment Maintenance	464	336	955	803	-15.92%	73.06%
Software Program Circulation	n/a	n/a	42,806	46,785	9.30%	n/a
Door Count	106,386	110,929	95,185	149,320	56.87%	40.36%

LEARNING RESOURCE SERVICES

LRS STRATEGIC PLANNING — PROCESS AND CHRONOLOGY

Strategic Plan Review

We anticipate a formal reevaluation and revision of the LRS Strategic Plan every five years. The proces to reevaluate the LRS Strategic Plan will begin in the spring of 1996 with a revision projected for publication in the summer 1997.

Austin Community College, Learning Resource Services, Strategic Plan, 1992. p.18

An LRS Strategic Planning Group — W.Lee Hisle, Toma Iglehart, Margaret Peloquin, Richard Smith — was organized to oversee the planning process.	April 1996

Three types of user surveys were designed and implemented:
    LRS Customer Survey (distributed in the LRCs)
    Faculty Survey (mailed to full-time and adjunct faculty)
    Student Survey (conducted in the classroom)
	Spring 1996

The Planning Group meets and designs a general process and timeline for LRS strategic planning.	May 1996
Representatives from all areas of LRS meet in a brainstorming session led by staff from ACC Institutional Effectiveness Office.	July 1996
The Planning Group meets to analyze and organize data from the brainstorming meeting. Preliminary mission and goals are defined.	July 1996
Representatives from all areas of LRS meet to review the preliminary mission and goals, make additional suggestions, and refine and prioritize issues identified in the July meeting.	August 1996

The Planning Group meets to analyze and organize data from the August meeting. Strategic Objectives are developed for FY98. The mission and goals are revised.	September 1996
The LRS Management Team reviews mission and goals, the FY98 strategic objectives, and defines budgetary objectives for FY98.	September / October 1996
All LRS professionals meet to review the draft mission and goals and the budgetary objectives for FY98.	November 1996
Strategic Planning Group and the LRS Management Team define assessment criteria for the ACC effectiveness survey of employees and students.	November 1996
The Strategic Planning Process is presented and the draft mission and goals are discussed at the annual All-LRS meeting. The mission and goals (1998-2002) are adopted in principle.	January 1997
The Planning Group analyzes data from the ACC effectiveness survey and correlates the information with the criteria defined.	February / March 1997
The Planning Group analyzes data from the Spring LRS surveys of faculty and students.	March / April 1997
The Planning Group meets with a Student Focus Group and an ACC Faculty/Staff Focus Group to identify issues. The focus groups also review the draft mission and goals and offer suggestions.	April 1997
The LRS Management Team reviews the results of the survey analyses and focus group meetings and suggests additional issues to be addressed by the strategic plan. LRS Mission and Goals (1998-2002) are adopted and the LRS vision is discussed.	April 1997

Representatives from all areas of LRS meet to review issues previously defined, suggest new issues, and prioritize issues to be used to create strategic objectives 1999-2002.	May 1997
The Planning Group meets to develop strategic objectives for 1999-2002..	June / July 1997
The Planning Group develops a draft outline of the strategic plan for review by the LRS Management Team.	June 1997
The Planning Group develops a preliminary draft of the strategic plan.	July 1997
The LRS Management Team and the ACC Academic Council review the preliminary draft.	July 1997
All LRS professionals review a final draft of the strategic plan.	August 1997
The LRS Strategic Plan for 1998-2002 is published.	August 1997

Shatford Library
Library Technology Master Plan
1997-2001

Submitted by

Mary Ann Laun
Assistant Dean, Library Services
Pasadena City College
February 1, 1998

Table of Contents

Introduction

Technologies are continuing to have a dynamic impact on the roles of librarians, libraries, and services to meet the information needs of students. As students' skills increase in the electronic arena, their capabilities for access to information resources increases exponentially and well beyond the traditional walls of libraries. This master plan addresses the four fundamental goals of this information technology plan:

Information Resources

The library will continue to provide PCC students with access to information resources that support their learning and intellectual needs, whether students are in the Shatford Library, at the CEC, elsewhere on campus, or off campus. The same commitment is made to faculty and staff to support their teaching and curricular needs. The library will also seek to facilitate easier access to information resources for residents of the district, and especially for students of the feeder high schools.

Instructional Arena

The librarians will continue to provide students with instruction and assistance, enabling them to integrate appropriate information resources into their educational objectives. Further collaboration with the PCC faculty will enhance training and assistance for the integration of information resources into faculty curricular, teaching, and scholarship interests. Along with the capability to access these expanding resources comes the responsibility to expand library instruction objectives to provide students with information competencies in the use of resources. These competencies may include but are not limited to the following:

- Ability to recognize that accurate and complete information is the basis for intelligent decision making
- Ability to recognize the need for information
- Ability to formulate questions based on information need
- Ability to identify and evaluate the credibility of sources of information
- Ability to find, access, and retrieve sources of information, using basic computer applications
- Ability to select and reject information within the context of a specific information need
- Ability to organize information for practical application
- Ability to synthesize and integrate new information into an existing body of knowledge
- Ability to use information in critical thinking and problem solving
- Ability to recognize and observe the rights to intellectual property as protected by copyright statutes.

— adapted from the National Forum on Information Literacy, Summary of Findings, 1992

Infrastructure

The library's role as an information delivery center is reliant on a strong infrastructure that enables the library to deliver resources beyond traditional hours and settings. The library needs to feel confident that telecommunication lines will provide reasonable response time. Cooperative efforts in networking with area libraries and feeder high schools will be explored.

Human Resources

The role of the librarian as a key facilitator in the integration of new technologies will be achieved through increased collaboration with discipline-based faculty. Human resources in the Shatford Library will need reassessment in order to assure effective instruction in the technological environment. Human resources in Campus Computing will need augmentation in order to support changing technology needs. All library staff will continue to be responsive to the increasingly diverse cultural and learning styles and circumstances of the library's users.

With a clear direction toward the mission of the college and the mission of the library, the library is dedicated to moving forward towards a greater utilization of resources by students. These four goals and integral strategies are directed to the achievement of greater integration of technology into the curriculum.

Pasadena City College

Mission Statement for the Shatford Library

The Shatford Library is committed to providing quality services for Pasadena City College's diverse community and the residents of the Pasadena Area Community College District. The librarians and library staff strive to:

Provide prompt, unbiased, and knowledgeable responses to requests for assistance, placing student and faculty information needs above other library and campus responsibilities;

Encourage and facilitate information competency, critical thinking, intellectual independence, and lifelong learning skills in all students, regardless of their educational goals (transfer, vocational and occupational, basic skills, noncredit education, or personal interest).

Provide quality instructional services and programs in the use of information resources and in support of the college's curriculum;

Promote the Shatford Library as the focal point of quality information resources, regardless of format, for the college community;

Provide professionally qualified librarians and a skilled technical staff that support the use of information in learning;

Ensure a comfortable and safe learning environment for all students;

Administer fair and objective service policies;

Provide assistance and access of collections and services to persons with special needs;

Protect each individual's right to privacy with respect to information requested and materials consulted;

Affirm the vision and mission of Pasadena City College.

3

Goals and Strategies

Goal 1: Information Resources

◆ Provide PCC students with access to information resources that support their learning and intellectual needs, whether students are in the Shatford Library, at the CEC, elsewhere on campus, or off campus.

◆ Provide PCC faculty with access to information resources that support their teaching and curricular needs. Support will be provided regardless of their location in the Shatford Library, at the CEC, elsewhere on campus, or off campus.

◆ Facilitate access to information resources for residents of the district, and especially for students of the feeder high schools.

Strategies:

Universal Online Access to Information Resources

Provide all students of Pasadena City College with wider dissemination of standardized online access to core resources, as identified by the librarians. These include, but are not limited to the following: online catalog of Shatford Library's book, media, and pamphlet collections, access to a core collection of academic journals and newspapers in full text, and a basic Reference collection (e.g. Microsoft Bookshelf).

Budgetary implications:

✓ Migration to UNIX platform that supports delivery of resources over the Web

✓ Enhancement of existing VTLS software to a web gateway (WebZ option)
(Note: Requires migration to MPE 5.5, VTLS 1.13, PERL, and gateway software)

✓ Designation of an electronic resources budget that supports institutional needs

✓ Upgrade or purchase of a library automation system with greater capabilities for information and networking

Organization of Effective Access to Electronic Resources

Make maximum use of national standards, protocols, and practices relative to electronic resources. Insure issues of confidentiality, security, and equal access. Expand current offerings to assure access to resources regardless of locality.

Budgetary implications:

✓ Z39.50 server software (and WebZ software) that allows greater access and flexibility between online systems

✓ Upgrade workstations to systems that can accommodate Web access and delivery

Design of the Shatford Library Web Page
Budgetary implications:

✓ Release time for development (hourly librarians)

Increased Access to Knowledge and Information Resources Outside of PCC

Currently interlibrary loan is underutilized by students due to cost and time restraints. Document delivery

4

is an option that the library staff has minimally explored. Investigate a user-initiated interlibrary loan and document delivery system to provide assistance in locating and obtaining materials that are difficult to obtain through the conventional interlibrary loan operations. Study cost recovery options to fund these resources.

Budgetary implications:

✓   Funding for an initial study year to determine needs assessment

Institutional Collaboration

Take an active part in statewide multitype library networks. Collaborate with other institutions (middle school through university level) to provide wider access to resources. Work with the CSU system to insure consortium purchase agreements not only for Pasadena City College but for the entire community college system as well.

Budgetary implications:

✓   Resource funding

Digitization and Imaging of PCC Resources

Cooperate with campus departments to identify archival and instructional resources that are appropriate for digitization and electronic delivery. Scope of these collections may include archival resources that are facing deterioration (e.g. Courier), electronic access to resources currently "protected," and electronic reserve room resources that provide additional access to students outside the college's physical boundaries. (Art slides and Nursing reserve resources are a prime candidate, pending copyright considerations.)

Budgetary implications:

✓   Evaluate and purchase hardware to digitize collections for increased access

✓   Acquire appropriate software to load these digitized images for Web access

Goal 2: Instructional Resources

* Provide PCC students with instruction and assistance enabling them to integrate appropriate information resources into their educational objectives.

* Collaborate with PCC faculty to provide training and assistance for the integration of information resources into their curricular, teaching, and scholarship interests.

Strategies:

Information Competency
Library faculty, discipline-based faculty, and professional and technical staff in disciplines will collaborate to determine the information competence needs of PCC students. In consultation with PCC's high schools and CSU campuses, strategies will be recommended to assure that students meet basic information skills. Assessment strategies should also be developed.

Budgetary implications:
✓   Library faculty to support additional responsibilities for instruction in these areas

Instructional Modules and Courses
Design and implement instructional credit modules in information competence for a diverse student body. Traditional and electronic instructional modules will be developed. Multi-campus representatives (from feeder high schools and high rate transfer institutions) could work collaboratively to develop information competency standards as well as instructional modules that meet the wide range of students' needs and backgrounds.

Budgetary implications:
✓   Release time for curriculum development
✓   Explore grant options for instructional improvement across institutions

Continuing Education for Discipline Faculty
Provide opportunities for all discipline faculty to update their library and research skills.

Budgetary implications:
✓   Library faculty to support additional responsibilities for instruction in these areas
✓   Staff development funds and flex day programs to support this need

6

Goal 3: Infrastructure

♦ Provide an infrastructure that will support the physical and access requirements of the students, faculty and staff of the 21st century.

♦ Guarantee telecommunication lines that will provide reasonable response time.

♦ Provide the capabilities for expansion for networking with area libraries and feeder high schools.

Strategies:

Facilities
Develop functional space for librarians and staff to train and assist students and faculty in their use of resources. This will involve formal classroom instruction as well as one-on-one or group instruction. Space for individual and team study areas will facilitate collaborative study and interaction between students, faculty and staff.

Equipment
Workstations should be upgraded to provide access to support the full utilization of print, recorded sound, graphic and electronic resources. A plan for replacement of equipment will be developed to avoid obsolescence. Plan to acquire ADA workstations to support students with disabilities.

Networking
The Shatford Library will link with the campus and CEC resources as well as with resources within the region, state, national and international networks. The value of networking with the feeder high schools has unlimited potential as students' information skills are enhanced. The value to recruitment efforts are also significant.

Budgetary implications:
▶ To be developed

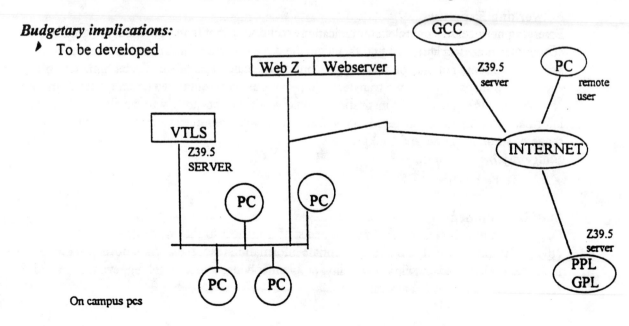

Goal 4: Human Resources

- Expand the role of the librarian in the teaching and learning process through the use of new information, networking, and instructional technologies and through increased collaboration with discipline-based faculty.

- Develop human resources in the Shatford Library to assure effective functioning in the evolving information and technological environments.

- Develop human resources in Campus Computing to support changing technology needs.

- Insure that library staff are responsive to the increasingly diverse cultural and learning styles and circumstances of the library's users.

Strategies:

Role of the librarians

With the explosion of available information and the increasingly diverse tools for access to that information, students' needs for instruction on gaining access to and using information is becoming more critical. This strategy seeks to develop an expanded role for librarians which can meet this need through the use of emerging information technologies.

Traditionally, librarians have taken a proactive approach in working with discipline-based faculty to develop appropriate information seeking skills for students. It is important to remember that information competency standards in our students implies information competency in our faculty and staff.

Budgetary implications:

✓ Flexible staffing options such as use of part-time librarians and staff, flex time, variable work schedules, and work-at-home program options may facilitate some of the preparatory changes to be made.

Networking Expertise

Emerging networking and telecommunications technology holds the potential for greater collaboration among librarians and faculty in the development of information competency skills for students not only on this campus, but on the campuses of our feeder high schools and the campuses to which we transfer. Multi-campus representatives (from feeder high schools and high rate transfer institutions) could work collaboratively to develop information competency standards as well as instructional modules that meet the wide range of students' needs and backgrounds.

Budgetary implications:

✓ To be developed

Staff Development

Ongoing technical training for librarians and staff is critical so that students can be guided effectively and efficiently toward appropriate information resources. Skill development includes technical updates, adaptability, flexibility, problem solving, critical thinking, evaluation and responsible, ethical use of information.

Shatford Library Technology Plan
Implementation and Funding

Timetable -- Revised February 1, 1998

Phase One -- Immediate	1997/ 1998	1998/ 1999	1990/ 2000	2000/ 2001	2000/ 2002	Funding Issues
Provide access to full text journals for CEC students	✓					
Install hub so that additional workstations can be added for library resources	✓					
Upgrade Internet lines to insure adequate response	✓					
Identify and map all possible network connections in the library for planning purposes	✓					
Purchase multimedia PC research station with jukebox (6-12) for single use reference resources	✓					
Upgrade all library staff computers for the transition to web based environment	✓					
Upgrade Jenny to a UNIX compatible system to support Web-delivery of library resources	✓					
Purchase VTLS web gateway as an intermediate step	✓					
Evaluate current library software options to explore the best long-term solution for delivery of library services	✓					

Task		
Purchase upgrade to library computer system after the evaluation of current library software options to explore the best long-term solution for delivery of library services	✓	
Convert CD-ROM resources to web subscriptions		✓
Upgrade all library public access computers for the transition to web based environment		✓
Purchase the Z39.50 software to allow communication between various online systems (at high schools, neighboring libraries and other institutions) Note: may defer to new online upgrade.		✓
Plan for integrating Shatford Library resources with neighboring libraries (array searches with Pasadena Public/Glendale Public and Glendale College)		✓
Provide a bridge to feeder high schools so that PCC's library resources can be searched locally		✓

Phase Three -- Long Term

	1997/1998	1998/1999	1999/2000	2000/2001	2001/2002	
Convert room adjacent to third floor Instruction Room to a multipurpose instructional lab and study area; recessed PCs with network and Internet connections offer this flexibility				✓		U
Evaluate and purchase hardware to digitize image collections for increased access (Art slide collection, Courier, PCC archival resources)			✓			U
Acquire appropriate software to load these digitized images for web access			✓			C P
Circulating laptop PCs for student home use			✓			C

Other Equipment Needs

Updated opaque overhead projector for Orientation Room		✓	
Automated Inventory control		✓	

Appendix A
Rationale for Migration to UNIX System

VTLS, the library's automation system has proven to be a reliable system, however after 14 years, it is now hardware and software that needs to be updated. The library staff is in the process of evaluating current needs in consideration of VTLS, as well as examining the numerous other options available today. In any case, a migration to a UNIX, which is becoming an industry standard, that allows server software will enable greater access to electronic resources over the Internet.

All contemporary systems have client-based or Web-interface software with graphical user interfaces. Networking between libraries utilizes the Web gateway software and the Z39.50 software to ease searches between systems. Of particular importance to the library's applications is the delivery of the library's databases over the Internet. This includes the library's catalogs, electronic reference resources, and periodical collections in full text. This is consistent with the college's goals to provide services to extended campus sites and to students' homes.

Equally important to this special needs request are the accreditation plans as cited in Standard 5:
5A.1 The Library and Learning Resources areas will identify the impact of new technologies on staffing, equipment, resources, and supplies and present special needs requests within the budget process.

5C.2 The Library and the CEC will study the library needs of students at the new Community Education Center and design a plan for off-campus library services and delivery. Note: The delivery of electronic resources to students at home, in labs, and at the CEC is an integral component of this recommendation.

FLORIDA STATE BOARD OF COMMUNITY COLLEGES

Office of Educational Services and Research

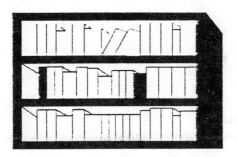

Library/Learning Resource Centers
Program Review
June 1997

**PROGRAM REVIEW
OF THE
FLORIDA COMMUNITY COLLEGE SYSTEM
Libraries/Learning Resource Centers**

TABLE OF CONTENTS

PROGRAM REVIEW
OF THE
FLORIDA COMMUNITY COLLEGE SYSTEM
Libraries/Learning Resource Centers

Executive Summary

This is the Level III Program Review of the Florida Community College System's Libraries and Learning Resource Centers commissioned by the Florida State Board of Community Colleges (SBCC) in keeping with Florida Statutes and SBCC policy. This study provides a better understanding of the roles Libraries and Learning Resource Centers (LRCs) programs should play in Florida's community colleges, identifies strengths and weaknesses of the current programs, and offers recommendations which will improve the ability of the programs to provide and support instruction--and thus improve the lives of students--in the Florida community colleges.

The following research questions formed the basis for the research.

1.   **What is the role and function of Libraries and Learning Resource Centers (LRCs) in community colleges?**

2.   **What services currently exist in libraries and LRCs? What services are needed to carry out the role and function of LRCs?**

3.   **What are the resources required to carry out the role and function of libraries/LRCs? What do we have? What do we need? What would we like to have?**

4.   **What external factors affect the capacity of the libraries/LRCs to achieve their role and function?**

5.   **What are the appropriate funding mechanisms to assure the resources required to carry out the role and function of libraries/LRCs are provided?**

6.   **What are the appropriate planning and evaluation mechanisms needed to enable the libraries/LRCs to achieve their proper role and function?**

STUDY DESIGN

The Program Review study design collected both quantitative data, through survey research, as well as qualitative information, through structured interviews and site visits.

All 28 community colleges in the Florida system were included in the study. Only cumulative scores by type of respondent, showing trends, were compiled from the survey research. No effort has been made to identify differences between college responses in the report.

Five colleges were selected to provide comprehensive survey data from six groups of respondents: Presidents; Vice-Presidents (who supervise the L/LRC Leader); Classroom Faculty; L/LRC Faculty and Staff; Students; and L/LRC Leaders (Directors. Deans, Associate VPs). These colleges were selected to represent a range of types and locations of institutions, from small, rural colleges to large, urban colleges. These colleges also were selected to host site visits by the Consultant. All other colleges were asked to survey only the President, the Vice-President, the L/LRC Faculty and Staff, and the L/LRC Leader. In addition, draft recommendations were reviewed and refined by the Council on Instructional Affairs and the Council of Presidents.

MAJOR FINDINGS

Purpose of L/LRC Programs

L/LRC programs are and will remain committed to supporting the educational mission of the parent institution. Central to the L/LRC mission is support for the college curriculum.

A continued need was expressed for quality traditional L/LRC services, such as reference, library instruction, media services, and maintaining a strong collection of resources. Many respondents pointed out that electronic information is not a panacea for their college's information needs. Traditional services, delivered by knowledgeable, courteous, and helpful staff, retains importance in any library/learning resources program of the future.

Staff

L/LRC staff knowledge, helpfulness, and commitment to student needs are viewed as among the strongest aspects of the L/LRC programs. This perception is held by all groups surveyed or interviewed during the site visits. Staff were mentioned regularly as helpful and knowledgeable; this is obviously a general strength throughout the state. All groups think there are too few staff members relative to need, especially in the area of instructional technology.

Materials Collections

The currency of materials collections is a major problem at many colleges. All groups surveyed and visited referred to the lack of a quality collection as a significant problem area. (The CCLA/Perrault, De Pew study mentioned in Section V indicates a seriously out-dated materials collection across the state: only 33 percent of the materials in community college collections statewide were published after 1980. Over 35 percent were published prior to 1970.)

Technology

Technology is generally recognized as the most important change-agent in L/LRC programs. The impact of technology on L/LRC programs is discussed in many areas throughout the study. For example, all respondents desired more access to the Internet/Web. Computing equipment accessibility was also a common concern. The faculty surveyed are aware of technology and understand its increasing importance but are concerned with lack of funding and progress in the implementation of technology at their campuses.

An area of agreement on a future role of L/LRC programs was the integration of technology into the instructional program, either through training or through use of electronic resources. Due to the complexity of electronic sources, students and faculty need critical-thinking skills to use electronic information sources effectively and intelligently.

Respondents agreed that traditional services, e.g., reference services, book and materials collection maintenance, would continue but would be supplemented by services to enhance technology in teaching and learning. Distance education was mentioned several times as a current and future activity which the L/LRC program will support.

Hours

Hours of operation were mentioned as a significant problem among students on the site visits and in their surveys. Hours are related to staff availability in that, usually, more staff are needed to extend library hours. The need for weekend hours of operation and Friday hours during the summer was voiced repeatedly.

Funding

All groups agreed that state appropriation is the "most appropriate" method for funding. Other methods of funding, such as a student fee for L/LRC programs, a technology fee, and fee-based services, were also thought to be worth consideration.

College Center for Library Automation (CCLA)

The CCLA was praised by all groups at all colleges, from presidents to students. Criticism by students was only heard regarding the difficulty of obtaining the materials identified as available on LINCC.

COMMITMENT TO EXCELLENCE

The twenty-eight Florida community colleges have demonstrated a commitment to excellence by adhering to criteria established by the Commission on Colleges of the Southern Association of Colleges and Schools (SACS). All of the colleges currently hold valid accreditation status. As part of its accreditation criteria, SACS places emphasis on institutional effectiveness measures with regard to library services rather than relying simply on the number of holdings as an indicator of quality. The SBCC should assure that the 28 local colleges have the necessary resources and support to successfully meet the SACS criteria related to Libraries and Learning Resource Centers. The 1994 Standards for Community, Technical, and Junior College Learning Resource Programs, developed by the Association of College and Research Libraries (ACRL), serve as useful guidelines the colleges may utilize in developing their Libraries/Learning Resources Programs.

RECOMMENDATIONS (ABRIDGED)

1. **Library/Learning Resource Center programs should have a Strategic Plan outlining their mission, goals, operational objectives, and evaluation methods. Such a strategic plan should be an integral part of the Institutional Effectiveness process required by SACS Criteria.**

2. **The State Board of Community Colleges should assure that the new Performance Based Program Budgeting System adequately addresses the continuing need for printed materials as well as recognizes the growing impact of the cost of electronic resources.**

3. **If program review implementation funding becomes available in 1998, it is recommended that a portion of those funds be used to support a non-recurring expenditure to improve and update the printed holdings in the community college libraries. Long term library support is an integral part of a college's base and categorical support should not become an ongoing budget strategy.**

4. **A system of materials delivery should be funded allowing statewide overnight access to resources from any college library.**

vii

5.   Libraries/Learning Resource Centers should become campus and college centers for access to electronic information and technology, including access to the Internet and Web, for all faculty, staff and students.

6.   The State Board of Community Colleges and the Florida Legislature should retain its commitment to the College Center for Library Automation as one of the strongest features of the Florida Community College System library/learning resources programs.

7.   To the degree that funding will allow, efforts at the local level should be made to assure that Libraries/Learning Resource Centers are in full compliance with the Criteria of the Commission on Colleges of SACS.

8.   Every effort should be made to provide services to students on days and at times such services are needed. The CCLA proposal related to an 800 number support system at times when the college is not able to be open will greatly respond to requests for additional hours on weekends.

9.   Colleges which offer distance education options should provide support for those students and faculty involved.

10. Community colleges should recognize that L/LRC services are an institution-wide resource which requires effective coordination and collaboration within multi-campus institutions in order to achieve commonly held goals.

STATISTICAL REPORTS

Annual/Monthly Summaries
Austin Community College
Central Florida Community College
West Valley College
Bunker Hill Community College
Reference Tally Form
Central Florida Community College

Summary of LRS Statistics

	1995-1996	1996-1997	Change
General LRS			
Door Count (All LRCs)*	886,067	821,143	-7%
Materials Circulation (All Formats)*	306,227	290,814	-8%
Total Volumes (All Formats)**	123,063	127,437	4%
Book Volumes Owned**	109,947	111,136	1%
Audiovisual Units Owned**	9,772	10,775	10%
Computer Software Units Owned**	3,443	4,225	23%
Subscriptions***	2,205	3,004	36%
Reference Transactions*	62,641	55,087	-12%
Students in Formal Instruction	12,122	10,258	-15%
Faculty/Staff in LRS Workshops	178	673	278%
Fees/Fines Collected*	54,944	52,717	-4%
Interlibrary Loans	459	386	-16%
Media Centers			
Door Count	148,021	153,632	4%
Production (All Media: Units)	8,766	7,763	-11%
Equipment Circulation	11,558	14,188	23%
Computer Centers			
Door Count	149,320	156,913	5%
Software Program Circulation	46,785	45,597	-3%

	CYP	ERG	NRG	PIN	RGC	RVS	ROB	****TOTAL
Statistics by Location FY 97								
Door Count	55,919	35,132	274,763	63,152	193,732	175,482	22,963	821,143
All Circulation	18,680	5,387	93,678	26,468	69,798	71,954	4,849	290,814
Reference Questions	4,159	4,577	16,706	5,985	12,612	10,166	882	55,087
Students in Library Instruction	645	390	2,088	525	4,706	1,671	233	10,258
Classroom Presentations	79	20	36	31	91	34	13	304
Students at Presentations	553	240	938	434	1,737	607	133	4,642
Fines/Fees	$1,736	$329	$18,895	$2,021	$15,643	$12,949	$1,143	$52,717
Square Footage	2,369	3150	9,914	3,541	10,326	11,500	2,324	43,124
Seating	53	62	163	72	237	201	28	816
Open Hours/Week	55	55	90	56	76	74	52	458
Reference Hours/Week	55	55	84	56	70	70	52	442

* RGC LRC had reduced facilities and collections for over four months due to construction. Several other statistical categories are affected by this as well.

** In FY 97, collection figures were recalculated electronically to increase accuracy.

*** FY 97 figures include microform and full text periodical subscriptions.

**** These totals do not include evening sites (Fredericksburg, San Marcos, Bastrop and Round Rock High School).

11/5/97 4:04 PM

Austin Community College

LRS Statistics by Location (FY97)

Location	Sq Ft (1)	Circ (2)	Circ/Hour (3)	Staff FTE (4)	Circ/Staff	Student FTE (5)	Circ/Student FTE	Users (6)	Users/Hour (7)
CYP	2,369	18,680	7.72	4.9	3,812	1,307	14.29	55,919	23.11
ERG	3,250	5,387	2.23	3.3	1,632	219	24.60	35,132	14.52
NRG	9,914	93,678	23.66	17.7	5,293	5,115	18.31	274,763	69.38
PIN	3,541	26,468	10.74	6.5	4,072	1,420	18.64	63,152	25.63
RGC	10,326	69,798	20.87	18.5	3,773	4,233	16.49	193,732	57.93
ROB	2,324	4,899	2.14	2.5	1,960	132	37.11	22,963	10.04
RVS	11,500	71,954	22.10	15.3	4,703	3,677	19.57	175,482	53.89
Total or Avg	43,224	290,864	12.78	68.70	4233.83	16,103	18.06	821,143	36.36

Location	Reference Questions (8)	Questions/Hour (9)	Lib FTE (10)	Ques/Lib FTE (11)	Volumes (12)	Volumes /Student	Seats (13)	Students /Seat
CYP	4,159	1.72	1.5	2,773	3,919	3.0	53	24.7
ERG	4,577	1.89	0.3	15,257	4,847	22.1	62	3.5
NRG	16,706	4.22	4.4	3,797	34,507	6.7	163	31.4
PIN	5,985	2.43	2	2,993	5,811	4.1	72	19.7
RGC	12,612	3.77	4.5	2,803	40,040	9.5	237	17.9
ROB	882	0.39	0.5	1,764	6,687	50.7	28	4.7
RVS	10,166	3.12	3.7	2,748	23,716	6.4	201	18.3
Total or Avg	55,087	2.51	16.90	3260	119,527(14)	7.42	816	19.73

(1) Square footage includes libraries, media, and computer centers, measured 7/97.

(2) Circulation: Dynlx materials, in all formats, checked out in FY97.

(3) Clr/Hours = Circ/44 Weeks/Hours open per week

(4) Staff FTE: All staff except student workers, FY97.

(5) Students FTE: Figures based on ACC Office of Institutional Research, FY97.

(6) Users: Gate count for all LRC units, FY97.

(7) Users/Hour = Users/44 Weeks/Hours open per week.

(8) Questions: Reference and informational questions, FY97.

(9) Questions/Hour=Ques/44 Weeks/Hours open per week

(10) Staffing table librarians plus FTE hourly librarians

(11) Librarian FTE: Based on total librarian FTE, not hours on the reference desk, FY97.

(12) Volumes: Based on LRS Tech. Services statistics, materials in all formats, FY97.

(13) Seats:[Student seating in LRCs, counted 9/97, including reference and computer workstations, media carrels, Dynix Stations, etc.]

(14) Minimum Collection(ACRL Standards, 1994): 180,900 and 11.54 Volumes/Student

CFCC -- OCALA LEARNING RESOURCES STATISTICS

Service	FY93	FY94	FY95	FY96	FY97
Enrollments					
Headcount	5,900	5,919	5,995	6,330	6,271
FTE	3,360	3,431	3,470	3,770	3,781
Campus Resources -- Ocala					
Book Titles	51,118	61,364	62,164	47,590[1]	51,167
Book Volumes	61,537	63,391	64,215	54,594	54,491
Video/Media	1,541	1,648	1,848	1,859	2,155
Sound Recordings	5,185	5,235	5,235	0	0
Magazine Titles	352	325	559	340	367
Access Services -- Processing					
Book Titles Added	969	451	1,528	1,643	2,875
Book Volumes Added	1,269	1,043	1,740	1,793	3,491
Videos Added	108	102	200	11	99
Citrus County Campus Retroconversion Project -- Data entry into LINCC					
Book Titles				Project began FY97	270
Book Volumes				Project began FY97	332
Videos				Not yet in process	0
Access Services -- Circulation					
Books Circulated	12,467	16,119	15,340	16,238	19,009[2]
Reserve Materials	4,572	3,013	4,330	4,241	5,165
Magazines	n/a	11,577	10,758	15,849	11,485[3]
Video/Media	372	585	1,137	1,352	1,594
Reference Services					
Reference Questions	5,017	6,268	5,255	16,277	15,244
Library Instruction					
Classes	n/a	11	36	68	67
Persons Attending	n/a	1,580	1,609	3,077	1,658[4]
Interlibrary Loan					
Materials Sent	0	4	9	4	16
Materials Borrowed	27	29	45	188	274
Media Services					
Equip. Distribution	519	458	227	376	408
Equipment Repair	404	341	391	583	623
AV Design Projects	5	4	6	24	38
Special Set-ups	n/a	157	288	507	142
Video Dubs	n/a	n/a	371	1,692	1,669
Audio Dubs	n/a	n/a	1,929	5,551	3,884
Video Prod/Taping	n/a	n/a	96	290	80
Photography	n/a	n/a	n/a	3,616	3,792
Teleconferences	1	32	35	131	72

[1] Decrease in book collection title and volume counts reflect shift from manual to CCLA database count.
[2] Increase reflects the acquisition of current, relevant titles and the implementation of CCLA circulation module.
[3] Decrease reflects the end of the New Student Orientation magazine assignment and the addition of full-text databases available through LINCC.

Central Florida Community College

FY Budget Closeouts

14101056   Library -- Ocala

Budget Category	FY92	FY93	FY94	FY95	FY96	FY97	FY98
Personnel Totals	226,560	211,800	218,000	214,255	274,979	302,499	309,725
Travel	608	1,567	203	413	162	469	
Shipping/Postage	211	43	333	562	118	155	
Repairs/Service Contract	1,911	0	377	0	1,192	210	
Memberships (NEFLIN)	15	0	0	450	450	450	
Supplies/Ed Materials/Printing	7,121	2,658	2,702	12,185	3,994	12,030	
CD-ROM/Database/Computer	0	1,730	1,485	12,836	13,490	15,153	
Periodical Subscriptions	25,479	30,822	25,063	13,430	15,792	17,662	
Expense Totals	35,345	36,820	30,163	38,876	35,198	46,129	45,590
Equipment	718	0	2,223	20,324	3,152	20,613	
Books	20,897	26,182	12,357	21,089	12,089	79,903	
Microfilm	5,009	0	0	3,814	3,951	6,624	
Videos	40	0	0	0	26	9,907	
Permanent Structure	0	0	0	0	0	338	
Capital Outlay Totals	26,664	26,182	14,580	45,227	19,218	117,395	85,000
Library Totals	288,569	274,802	262,743	298,358	329,395	466,023	440,315

Central Florida Community College

CFCC -- OCALA LEARNING RESOURCES DEPARTMENT
Monthly Statistics March, 1998

Service	FY 97	FY97-Date	FY98-Date	Mar-97	Mar-98
Resources Processed -- Ocala					
Book Titles Added	2,875	2,379	2,217	428	195
Book Titles Withdrawn	495	390	355	0	75
Book Volumes Added	3,491	2,913	2,534	576	207
Book Volumes Withdrawn	782	641	295	0	113
Videos Added	99	4	383	0	92
Videos Withdrawn	0	0	0	0	0
Microfilm Added	40	26	40	0	0
Video Retroconversion	0	0	804	0	66
Resources Processed into LINCC -- Citrus		0			
Book Titles Added	236	n/a	2,435	n/a	105
Book Titles Withdrawn	0	n/a	2	n/a	0
Book Volumes Added	298	n/a	7,626	n/a	115
Book Volumes Withdrawn	0	n/a	0	n/a	0
Videos Added	0	n/a	253	n/a	127
Videos Withdrawn	0	n/a	0	n/a	0
Circulation Services					
Books Circulated	19,009	14,914	15,076	2,298	2,304
Reserves Circulated	5,165	4,171	4,575	296	416
Magazines Circulated	11,485	9,824	7,567	1,005	918
Videos/Media Circulated	1,352	1,270	866	125	103
Microforms Circulated	604	617	411	71	37
Telecourses Distributed	193/$2417	0	412/3958	n/a	3/$11
Fine/Lost Book Receipts	1702/$382	0	1860/4580	n/a	208/$430
Reference Services					
Reference Questions	15,244	12,372	15,290	1,365	1,342
Instruction Classes/Students	67/1658.	134/1471	76/1633	3/65	3/47
Interlibrary Loan Shared	16	14	19	4	9
Interlibrary Loan Borrowed	274	224	368	26	54
Intralibrary Loan to Citrus	0	0	16	0	0
Intralibrary Loan from Citrus	0	0	2	0	0
Media Services					
Equipment Distribution	408	273	215	19	34
Equipment Repair	623	542	696	55	71
Special Set-ups	142	128	146	23	32
Video Duplication	1,669	1,239	2,375	325	100
Audio Duplication	3,884	3,582	7,484	421	30
Video Stenography/Taping	80	47	16	4	2
Photographs	3,792	2,166	3,562	261	300
Teleconferences	72	58	16	25	2

Special Notes: Please see reverse.

Stat Sheet Master Form

FISCAL YEAR 97-98	JULY	AUG	SEPT	OCT	NOV	DEC	JAN	FEB	MAR	APR	MAY	JUNE	FY TOTAL
Reference Services: Lynnette 1,2; Dave 3													
1 Reference Questions													
2 Directional Questions													
3 On-line database searches													
Book Circulation: Rosalie													
4 Books Checked Out													
5 Reserves Checked Out													
6 Other Items Checked Out													
7 Total Items Checked out													
8 In-house Use of Items													
9 TOTAL of #7 & #8													
Periodical Circulation: Patty													
10 Periodicals Circulation													
11 Microform Circulation													
12 Per./Microform Processing*													
*includes newspapers													
AV Circulation: Katy													
13 AV software checked out													
14 Computer Software													
15 Equipment													
16 TOTAL:													
ILL: Rosalie													
17 ILL requests made													
18 How many filled													
19 How many filled by:													
20 Calif. Comm. Colleges													
21 Calif. State Univ.													
22 Public													

Page 1

West Valley College

Stat Sheet Master Form

		JULY	AUG	SEPT	OCT	NOV	DEC	JAN	FEB	MAR	APR	MAY	JUNE	FY TOTAL
23	Other													
	How many were:													
24	Monographs													
25	Periodicals													
26	Government documents													
27	Public													
28	Other													
	ILL rec'd from others: Rosalie													
29	How many received													
30	How many filled for:													
31	Calif. Comm. Colleges													
32	Calif. State Univ.													
33	Univ. of Calif.													
34	Public													
35	Other													
36	How many were:													
37	Monographs													
38	Periodicals - Patty													
39	Gov't Documents													
40	Public													
41	Other (video)													
	Orientations: Lynnette													
42	Number of Orientations													
43	No. participating													
	Credit Courses: Bill													
44	Courses													
45	Sections													
46	No. students completed													

Page 2

West Valley College

Stat Sheet Master Form

	JULY	AUG	SEPT	OCT	NOV	DEC	JAN	FEB	MAR	APR	MAY	JUNE	FY TOTAL
47 #Patrons Using Lib.RH													
48 #Comm. Borrowers RH													
Books/Serials: Diane													
49 Books added (titles)													
50 Books added - (volumes)													
51 Books added gifts, (vol.)													
52 Bound period. added (vol)													
53 Vol. withdrawn/books and bound periodicals													
54 Reserves Withdrawn													
Periodicals/Newspapers: Sylvia													
55 Subscriptions added													
56 Microform subscriptions and microform standing orders added (titles)													
Microforms: Patty													
57 No. of film reels added													
58 No. of film titles added													
59 M/F other than reels added (no. of pieces)													
60 M/F other than reels added (no. of titles)													
Other Print items added: Diane (VIv. Item 62)													
61 Juvenile works (vols)													
62 Textbooks & other reserve materials (vols)													
(Continued on next page)													

Stat Sheet Master Form

	JULY	AUG	SEPT	OCT	NOV	DEC	JAN	FEB	MAR	APR	MAY	JUNE	FY TOTAL
63	Pamphlets (pieces) (LP)												
64	Other printed works, not fully cataloged												
	A/V Items Added: Vivian												
65	Audio recordings added, tapes, etc. (No. of titles)												
66	Audio recordings added, tapes, etc. (No. of items)												
67	Film and Video added (No. of titles)												
68	Film and video added (No. of items)												
69	Other audio-visual items added but not indicated above (indicate number, not titles)												
70	Total added												
71	Withdrawals of AV items												
	Computer Items: Vivian												
72	M/C software added (titles)												
73	M/C software total (copies)												
74	Compact Disk--Read-only Databases (titles)												
75	Deleted												
	Equipment added: Katy 76, 77, 79; Dave 78												
76	Audio equipment added												
77	Film and video added												
78	M/C equipment added												
79	Other A/V equipment:												

7/15/94 lp

Page 4

West Valley College

MONTH AT A GLANCE
LIBRARY REPORT*

Date of Report: _____

Period covered in this report: **FROM:** _____ **TO:** _____

Regular library schedule: M-TR 8:00am to 9:00pm, F 8:00am to 5:00pm & Saturday 9:00am to NOON (*64 hours* open to the public).

Variations in the regular library schedule effecting this report include:

_____
_____ (note schedule changes that effect
_____ the normal 64 hour schedule)

Total hours open to public reflected in this report are: _____

The BHCC Library was open _____ days, serving _____ patrons (exit gate count).

_____ **new patrons** were registered, _____ orientation and specialty *tours* were given with an attendance of _____. _____ *workshops* and focus classes were conducted with an attendance of _____.

InterLibraryLoan activity (includes NOBLE and other MA point to point libraries and OCLC): **ILL " IN ":** _____ **ILL " OUT ":** _____

Materials processed include (technical services area):

Pre-cataloged new items (new book and permanent collection items: _____
Cataloged items (donations & purchases): _____

EBSCO is only one of many databases accessed by BHCC library patrons noted in this report because it is representative of the average BHCC library user.

Total # of **EBSCO searches** this month: ____. The average # of **hits per search** _____.
Top three EBSCO titles retrieved: (#)_____
　　　　　　　　　　　　　　　　　　(#)_____
　　　　　　　　　　　　　　　　　　(#)_____

Reference Desk Transactions:
Reference Interviews conducted by ref. depart. and other staff members: _____.
Mechanical Transactions from the Reference Desk _____.

* See the procedure sheet for Month At A Glance Reports for entry clarification.

Procedure sheet: This sheet is to be used with blank forms titled <u>**MONTH AT A GLANCE LIBRARY REPORT**</u>* with the asterisk in reference to the following notation:* **See the procedure sheet... for entry clarification**

General Statistics Section: (see Diane Smith)
Check the front desk calendar for actual library hours for the month and the exit gate figures for the beginning and end of the month. Use the NOBLE month end statistical reports for the actual number of items checked in, checked out and the # of new patrons (see attached sample).

Tours and workshop figures are a combination of the daily calendar/desk calendar at the Reference desk and the daily calendar/desk calendar at the front desk. Orientation and specialty tours are more broadly scoped, information type, introductory sessions routinely conducted to address library user needs. Workshops and focus classes refer to more specialized custom sessions usually conducted with the involvement of a faculty member moving beyond information into the area of instruction, addressing specific student and/or faculty needs.

InterLibraryLoan Section:
The NOBLE figures are taken from the month end statistical reports. ILL IN are taken from Network From and ILL From and ILL OUT are taken from Network To and ILL To. The OCLC figures are taken from the OCLC ILL activity reports from Bob Kintz. Combine the NOBLE IN & OUT totals with the OCLC IN and OUT totals to reach the Total ILL IN and Total ILL OUT figures to be recorded on the Month At A Glance Report.

Technical Services Information: (see Lana Ordian materials processing and EBSCO)
Pre-cataloged items include the Baker and Taylor Book Lease Program (total count including even books that will be returned) and the new and replacement books the BHCC library purchases for the permanent collection. Cataloged items are all new and replacement books purchased by or donated to the BHCC library which are processed using NOBLE and OCLC system records as well as those which require original cataloging.

EBSCO figures are obtained in the administrative part of the EBSCO database.

Reference Desk Transactions: (see Diane Smith)
Reference Interviews are usually conducted by reference staff and a daily log (clipboard and file) is kept at the reference desk. Other staff members contribute routinely and should be reporting their activity on this same log. Mechanical transactions from the Reference Desk refers to more routine responses to library user questions and needs and are recorded daily on the same log.

NOTE: Keep only *month end* statistical records for the *current year*. Everything else may be discarded.

Bunker Hill Community College

1/30/98

LRC REFERENCE STATISTICS

DATE: _____

DAY: _____

HOURS	INFORMATIONAL	DIRECTIONAL	TOTALS
7:30 a.m. - 9:00a.m.			
9:00a.m. - 11:00a.m.			
11:00a.m. - 1:00p.m.			
1:00p.m. - 3:00p.m.			
3:00p.m. - 5:00p.m.			
5:00p.m. - 7:00p.m.			
7:00p.m. - 9:00p.m.			
TOTALS			

NOTES:

USER SATISFACTION SURVEYS

General User Surveys
Northwest Indian College
Indian River Community College
Imperial Valley College
Pasadena City College
Southern Ohio College
Technical College of the Lowcountry
De Anza College
Scottsdale Community College

Student Surveys
Central Florida Community College
Austin Community College
Elaine P. Nunez Community College

Faculty Surveys
Central Florida Community College
Schenectady Community College
Austin Community College
Corning Community College

Reference Service Survey
Central Florida Community College

Library Instruction Surveys
Technical College of the Lowcountry
Elaine P. Nunez Community College

Suggestion Box Form
Broome Community College

LIBRARY SURVEY FOR ACCREDITATION
IF YOU HAVE ALREADY FILLED ONE OUT-PLEASE RETURN TO INSTRUCTOR NOW.

Check items that describe you best: (you may select two)

☐ NWIC Student   ☐ NWIC Staff   ☐ NWIC Faculty

☐ I am on the main campus   ☐ I am at the _____ site.

I use the _____ Library-- ☐ Daily ☐ Weekly ☐ Monthly ☐ Other ☐ Never
        Name of Site
- **Please state a reason if your answer is Never.**

(Please disregard the rest of the questionnaire if you never use a library)

I (☐ Always, ☐ Usually, ☐ Often, ☐ Seldom, ☐ Never) **find what I am looking for in the library**.

I have used (or am aware of) the following in the library:

Used	Aware of		Used	Aware of	
[ ]	[ ]	CD-ROM Resources	[ ]	[ ]	Map Collection
[ ]	[ ]	Internet Resources	[ ]	[ ]	Special Collections Resources
[ ]	[ ]	Vertical File Resources	[ ]	[ ]	Overhead Projector
[ ]	[ ]	Magazine Resources	[ ]	[ ]	Computers for homework
[ ]	[ ]	Athena (the library's computerized card catalog)	[ ]	[ ]	Slide Projector
[ ]	[ ]	TV-VCR	[ ]	[ ]	Videos
[ ]	[ ]	WLN Interlibrary Loan Resources	[ ]	[ ]	Microfiche
[ ]	[ ]	Dictaphone Machine	[ ]	[ ]	Audio Tape Player
[ ]	[ ]	Laminator	[ ]	[ ]	Projector Screen
[ ]	[ ]	Xerox Machine (Coin Operated)	[ ]		

I usually use the library in:
☐ Morning   ☐ Afternoon   ☐ Tuesday Evening   ☐ Saturday Mornings

02/18/98

I think the library hours should be: ☐ Kept the same   ☐ expanded to include:
_____ (The library at
the Lummi Campus is currently open Mon., Wed., Thurs., and Fri. from 8:00 - 5:30. Tues.
8:00 - 8:00 and Sat. from 9:00 - 1:00).

I think the library has resource materials that are:
☐ Up-to-date   ☐ Fairly new   ☐ Old but useful   ☐ Old and out of date.

I have found the following subject areas need to have new, up-to-date materials:
_____, _____, _____, _____

I have ☐ Always   ☐ Often   ☐ Seldom   ☐ Never **found adequate study space in the
library.**

I am aware of the planning process for the library (Library Advisory Committee). ☐ Yes ☐ No

**(This committee is looking for participants- call Malinda Davidson at Extension 212, or the
library staff at extension 204 for more information.)**

....

The following questions concern the library staff. Please comment honestly as to how the
library staff has treated you. Please check as many as apply to your experiences while using
the library. You may comment at the conclusion of this section if you wish.

Professionalism: (Check all that apply)

☐ Very knowledgeable   ☐ Competent ☐ Well-Trained   ☐ Unapproachable
    ☐ Accessible   ☐ Needs more library training   ☐ Approachable
    ☐ Inaccessible   ☐ Helpful   ☐ Too busy to help me   ☐
Other_____.

The library staff is helping me to be more independent in the library by showing me how to :
☐ Find books using Athena (computer catalog program)   ☐ Use the Internet
☐ Use the following CD-ROM Resource(s) _____,
    _____, _____, _____,

GENERAL COMMENTS CONCERNING THE LIBRARY:

I think the library could improve in the following areas:
☐ Staff Training (Please add Suggestions)
☐

☐ Book Collection(s):

☐ Science   ☐ Health/Medical   ☐ History   ☐ Philosophy   ☐ Math   ☐ Psychology
☐ Sociology   ☐ Business   ☐ Literature   ☐ Education   ☐ Technology   ☐ Arts/Crafts

02/18/98

☐ Native American Material   ☐ Other _____, _____

How close is another library to you that you can use: _____miles.

This is a   ☐ Public   ☐ College   ☐ Tribal   ☐ Other _____library.

How does the facility where you attend NWIC compare with the other library facilities available to you?
(Specific comments would be helpful here)

Thank you for filling this survey out and for your comments. **If you are faculty, please continue.**
....

For Faculty Only:

I bring my class(es) in for library orientations: ☐ Always   ☐ Sometimes   ☐ Never
If never, please comment:

The library offers adequate, up-to-date resources in my discipline(s): _____,
(you may leave blank, but the discipline would help us access the library better)

☐ Yes   ☐ No   ☐ Some   ☐ Section should be weeded   ☐ Needs to be replaced

Topics/subjects that need more up-to-date coverage_____

The Library staff is willing to help my students find resources, including those I have put on reserve for them:..
☐ Yes   ☐ No   ☐ Sometimes   ☐ Never   ☐ I don't require my students to use the library.

I require my students to use the library by assigning:
☐ Research projects   ☐ Term Papers   ☐ Book Reports   ☐ Magazines article
☐ Abstracts   ☐ Bibliographies   ☐ Internet Searches   ☐ Other_____

Ways I think the library could be improved for my students. Please be specific.

Ways in which the library could be improved for the faculty. Please be specific.

02/18/98

IRCC Main Library Patron Satisfaction Survey, Part 1

We would like your impressions about the IRCC Main Library's service performance.

For each of the following statements, please indicate your perception of the Main Library's service by circling one of the numbers in the column.

When it comes to . . .	My Perception of the Library's Service Performance is:		
	Low	High	No Opinion
Q.1 Prompt service to customers	1 2 3 4 5 6 7 8 9		N
Q.2 Staff who are consistently courteous	1 2 3 4 5 6 7 8 9		N
Q.3 Staff who deal with customers in a caring fashion	1 2 3 4 5 6 7 8 9		N
Q.4 Providing service at the promised time	1 2 3 4 5 6 7 8 9		N
Q.5 Staff who understand the needs of their customers	1 2 3 4 5 6 7 8 9		N
Q.6 Visually appealing materials associated with the service (e.g., clear and concise forms)	1 2 3 4 5 6 7 8 9		N
Q.7 Having the customer's best interest at heart	1 2 3 4 5 6 7 8 9		N
Q.8 Willingness to help customers	1 2 3 4 5 6 7 8 9		N
Q.9 Maintaining error-free customer and catalog records	1 2 3 4 5 6 7 8 9		N
Q.10 Keeping customers informed about when services will be performed	1 2 3 4 5 6 7 8 9		N

When it comes to . . .	My Perception of the Library's Service Performance is:		
	Low High	No Opinion	
Q.11 Providing services as promised	1 2 3 4 5 6 7 8 9	N	
Q.12 Staff who instill confidence in customers	1 2 3 4 5 6 7 8 9	N	
Q.13 Staff who have the knowledge to answer patrons' questions	1 2 3 4 5 6 7 8 9	N	
Q.14 Readiness to respond to patrons' questions	1 2 3 4 5 6 7 8 9	N	
Q.15 Dependability in handling patrons' service problems	1 2 3 4 5 6 7 8 9	N	
Q.16 Performing services right the first time	1 2 3 4 5 6 7 8 9	N	
Q.17 Visually appealing facilities	1 2 3 4 5 6 7 8 9	N	
Q.18 Giving patrons individual attention	1 2 3 4 5 6 7 8 9	N	
Q.19 Staff who have a neat, professional appearance	1 2 3 4 5 6 7 8 9	N	
Q.20 Convenient business hours	1 2 3 4 5 6 7 8 9	N	
Q. 21 Modern equipment	1 2 3 4 5 6 7 8 9	N	
Q.22 Assuring patrons of the accuracy and confidentially of their transactions	1 2 3 4 5 6 7 8 9	N	

IRCC Main Library Patron Satisfaction Survey, Part 2

A. How would you rate the overall quality of the service provided by the IRCC Main Library?
(circle one number below)

Extremely Poor   **Extremely Good**

  1   2   3   4   5   6   7   8   9

B. Listed below are five general features pertaining to academic libraries and the services they offer. We would like to know how important a feature is to you when you evaluate an academic library's quality of services.

Please allocate a total of 100 points among the five features according to how important each feature is to you--the more important a feature is to you, the more points you should give to it. Please be sure the points you give add up to 100.

1. The appearance of the library's physical facilities, equipment,
   personnel, and communications materials.   _____ points

2. The library's ability to perform the promised services dependably
   and accurately.   _____ points

3. The library's willingness to help customers and provide prompt
   service.   _____ points

4. The knowledge and courtesy of the library's staff and their
   ability to convey trust and confidence   _____ points

5. The caring, individualized attention the library provides its customers.   _____ points

Total Points Allocated 100 points

Indian River Community College

IRCC Main Library Patron Satisfaction Survey, Part 3

This part of the survey is to gather some information about you as a library user. Please complete the following statements: (Circle one)

1. My affiliation with IRCC is :   Faculty   Staff   Student

2. I visit the IRCC Main Library: Daily   Weekly   Monthly   Never

3. These are some additional comments I have about the IRCC Main Library: _____

_____

_____

_____

_____

_____

_____

_____

Indian River Community College

SPENCER LIBRARY MEDIA CENTER USER SURVEY, SPRING, 1997

The Library staff wants to meet your needs. Please take a moment to answer these questions and let us know how we are doing. Please mark in pencil on the Scantron sheet the answer to each question.   If you have specific comments, please write them at the end of this survey and return it to the Library staff.

1. How often do you use the IVC Spencer Library Media Center?

     A. Daily   B. Weekly   C. Monthly   D. Rarely   E. Never.

2. Generally, when looking for information in the IVC Library, do you find the information you need?

     A. Yes   B. No   C. Partially

3. If you answered "no" or "partially", indicate the most common reason

     A. Couldn't find any information
     B. Information I needed was checked out or not available (missing, overdue, not on the shelf, etc.)
     C. Other

4. When looking for information in the IVC Library, is it easy to find?

     A. Yes   B. No   C. Sometimes

5. When you find information, how would you characterize it?

     A. Current   B. Too old   C. Just right

6. How would you describe the *quantity* of the information you find in the library?

     A. Too little   B. Too much   C. The right amount for my needs

7. How would you describe the *quality* of the information you find in the library?

     A. Too difficult or too scholarly
     B. Appropriate level
     C. Too easy or too popular

8. What is your most common use of the library?

     A. Class assignments   C. Job related interests   E. Other
     B. Personal interests   D. Study hall

9 Do you feel that the library is open enough hours to meet your needs?

      A. Yes   B. No   C. No opinion

10 Do you feel comfortable asking the library staff for assistance?

      A. Yes   B. No   C. No opinion

11. If no, why not?

      A. I like to help myself
      B. The library staff is too busy
      C. I don't know who to ask
      D. I am afraid to ask for help
      E. Other

12. When you ask for help, is the library staff helpful?

      A. Yes   B. No   C. Sometimes

13. How do you rate the electronic indexes of magazines and journals (e.g. ProQuest, SIRS, Infotrac)?

      A. Easy to use   B. Neither easy nor difficult   C. Difficult to use

14. Are there other things you would like the Library to offer?

      A. More books   C. More hours   E. Other
      B. More magazines   D. More computers

15. In general, how do you rate the library's services?

      A. Excellent   B. Good   C. Fair   D. Poor

Thank you for taking the time to complete this survey.

Pasadena City College Shatford Library User Survey

1. How often do you use the PCC Library?
   A.   daily or weekly
   B.   monthly
   C.   rarely
   D.   never

2. Generally, when looking for information in the Shatford Library, do you find information that you need?
   A.   yes
   B.   no
   C.   partially

3. If you answered "no" or "partially", indicate the most common reason.
   A.   Couldn't find any information
   B.   Information I needed was checked out or not available (e.g. missing, overdue, not on the shelf)
   C.   Other

4. When you find information, how would you characterize it?
   A.   current
   B.   too old
   C.   just right

5. How would you describe the *quantity* of the information you find in the library?
   A.   too little
   B.   too much
   C.   the right amount for my needs

6. How would you describe the *quality* of the information you find in the library?
   A.   too difficult or too scholarly
   B.   appropriate level
   C.   too easy or too popular

7. What is your most common use of the library?
   A.   class assignments
   B.   personal interests
   C.   job related interests
   D.   study hall
   E.   Other

8. Do you feel that the library is open long enough to meet your needs?
   A. yes
   B. no
   C. no opinion

9. Do you feel comfortable asking the librarian for assistance?
   A.   yes
   B.   no
   C.   no opinion

10. If no, why not?
    A.   I like to help myself
    B.   The librarian is too busy
    C.   I don't know where the librarian is
    D.   I am afraid to ask for help
    E.   Other (please specify on the back of this sheet)

11. Do you feel comfortable using the computers in the library?
    A.   yes
    B.   no
    C.   no opinion

12. How do you rate the library's computerized book catalog?
    A.   easy to use
    B.   neither easy nor difficult
    C.   difficult to use

13. How do you rate the electronic indexes of magazines and journals?
    A.   easy to use
    B.   neither easy nor difficult
    C.   difficult to use

14. In general, how do you rate PCC's library services?
    A.   Excellent
    B.   Good
    C.   Fair
    D.   Poor

For home comupter users:

15. Do you have a computer at home?
    A.   yes
    B.   no

16. If you have a computer, does it have a modem?
    A.   yes
    B.   no

17. Do you access the Internet at home?
    A.   yes
    B.   no

Southern Ohio College, Akron Campus Library Evaluation 1990

(1) I am _____ male _____ female,   (2) _____ student _____ faculty.

If a "student," I am   (3) _____ full time _____ part time.

and I left high school   (4) _____ before 1990 _____ after 1990.

(5) My major field of study here is _____.

(6) Check the number of times you have used the library for some reason in the last month.

_____(0)   _____(1-3)   _____(4-6)   _____(7-9)

(7) I use the library here at SOC for:
(check all that apply)
_____ books
_____ magazines
_____ videos or cassettes
_____ reference assistance
_____ Infotrac, the computerized index of magazine articles
_____ Internet searching
_____ a quiet place to study
_____ for student/teacher conferences
_____ _____

(8) What kind of BOOKS have you needed to find in this library that have not been there?

(9) What MAGAZINE titles have you needed for school work that we do not receive?

(10) Have you needed to go to another library in order to complete your class work?

(11) Name up to five magazines that you look at most frequently (if any.)

Thank you very much! Please return this form to your teacher or place it in the box provided in the library.

Technical College of the Lowcountry
Learning Resources Center
General Survey

1.   You are:
     ___ TCL Student   ___ TCL Staff   ___ Other
     ___ TCL Faculty   ___ USCB Student

2.   Your major or department (skip this question if it is not applicable):_____

3.   What did you do in the library today? (Circle the number that best reflects how successful the outcome was)

		Did not do today	Not at all				Completely
A.	Use the online catalog	0	1	2	3	4	5
B.	Look for books on the shelf	0	1	2	3	4	5
C.	Use Proquest	0	1	2	3	4	5
D.	Use Newsbank	0	1	2	3	4	5
E.	Use CINAHL	0	1	2	3	4	5
F.	Look for periodicals	0	1	2	3	4	5
G.	Use the reference collection	0	1	2	3	4	5
H.	Search or browse internet	0	1	2	3	4	5
I.	Ask a reference question	0	1	2	3	4	5

4.   Have you participated in an LRC orientation? ___ Yes ___ No

5.   What services would you like the LRC to add or improve? (please explain)

6.   In the appropriate box, please write the hours that are most convenient for you to use the LRC.

	Morning	Afternoon	Evening
Monday - Thursday			
Friday			
Saturday			
Sunday			

Please make any additional comments on back of this page so that the LRC may better serve you.

De Anza College Library

PLEASE HELP US IMPROVE LIBRARY SERVICE BY
ANSWERING A FEW QUESTIONS

1. What did you do in the library today? For each, circle the number that best reflects how successful you were.

	Successful?					
	Did not do today	Not at all				Completely
A. Checked out library books	0	1	2	3	4	5
B. Read library periodicals	0	1	2	3	4	5
C. Used the Open Media Lab	0	1	2	3	4	5
D. Used library computers to do research.	0	1	2	3	4	5
E. Asked for help from library staff.	0	1	2	3	4	5
F. Other(what?)___	0	1	2	3	4	5

2. How <u>easy</u> was the library to use <u>today</u>? (Circle one):

	1	2	3	4	5
	Not at all easy				Very easy

Why?_____

3. Overall, how <u>satisfied</u> are you with <u>today's</u> library visit? (Circle one):

	1	2	3	4	5
	Not at all satisfied				Very satisfied

Why?_____

4. Today's visit was primarily in support of (Check one):

__1. Course Work   __3. Teaching   __5. A mix of several purposes

__2. Research   __4. Current Awareness   __6. Other:_____

De Anza College

5. You are (Check one):

___1. De Anza Student/part time ___3. De Anza student/full time ___5 De Anza faculty/staff

___2. Student/staff - other college ___4. High school student or staff ___6. Other(what?)_____

6. Your research area today was (Check one):

___1. Arts ___3. Sciences ___5. Social Sciences ___7. Other (What?)_____

___2. Business ___4. Languages ___6. Technology

OTHER COMMENTS? Please use the space below.

Library Services Survey
We Would Like To Know What You Think

Our library staff wants to improve the services we offer you. Please take a moment to let us know how we are doing and how we can improve.

1. How satisfied are you with our books?
    ☐ Extremely　☐ Very　☐ Somewhat　☐ Not very　☐ Not at all

    With our magazines and journals?
    ☐ Extremely　☐ Very　☐ Somewhat　☐ Not very　☐ Not at all

    With our electronic resources?
    Infotrac/Searchbank?
    ☐ Extremely　☐ Very　☐ Somewhat　☐ Not very　☐ Not at all

    CD-ROMs (Readers' Guide Abstracts, New York Times Index, Arizona Republic, etc.)?
    ☐ Extremely　☐ Very　☐ Somewhat　☐ Not very　☐ Not at all

2. How helpful is our staff?
    ☐ Extremely　☐ Very　☐ Somewhat　☐ Not very　☐ Not at all

3. How easy is it to find what you need?
    ☐ Extremely　☐ Very　☐ Somewhat　☐ Not very　☐ Not at all

4. How important is the library to you?
    ☐ Extremely　☐ Very　☐ Somewhat　☐ Not very　☐ Not at all

5. How often do you visit the library or call for information?
    ☐ Weekly　☐ Monthly　☐ 4 times/year　☐ Twice/year　☐ Yearly

6. How often do you ask a librarian for help?
    ☐ Weekly　☐ Monthly　☐ 4 times/year　☐ Twice/year　☐ Yearly

7. Are there other things you would like the library to offer?
    ☐ More books　☐ More Magazines and Journals　☐ More reference materials
    Other _____

8. Are you a　☐ student　☐ faculty/staff　☐ other _____

We would like your comments and suggestions about how we can improve our services to you.

Thank you for taking time to comment.

Scottsdale Community College

LIBRARY/LEARNING RESOURCES DEPARTMENT
STUDENT USE SURVEY

The Library/Learning Resources staff is interested in learning about how often and for what reasons you use the library. Your response is important to us since the results will help us improve library/learning resources materials, facilities, and services. Thank you for your help.   <u>*PLEASE CIRCLE ALL DESIRED RESPONSES.*</u>

1. **Your major program is in**
   _____ Business
   _____ Communications/Fine Arts
   _____ Health Occupations
   _____ Humanities
   _____ Math. Science & Physical Ed
   _____ Public Service
   _____ Technical Education
   _____ Undecided

2. **How often do you use Library/ Learning Resources services?**
   _____ 2-5 times per week
   _____ 1-3 times per month
   _____ less than once a month
   _____ never

3. **How often do you use the following library/learning resources services?**
   (1=often, 2=sometimes, 3=not at all)

a.	Browsing magazines, newspapers, pleasure books	1	2	3
b.	Photocopying materials	1	2	3
c.	Researching for a paper or class project	1	2	3
d.	Studying, doing homework	1	2	3
e.	Surfing the Internet, e-mail, chat rooms	1	2	3
f.	Using reserve materials	1	2	3
g.	Viewing audiovisual materials	1	2	3
h.	Visiting with friends	1	2	3
i.	Working with my study group	1	2	3

4. **Do you find it easy to get help when you want it for**
   (1=always, 2=sometimes, 3=never, 4=not wanted)

a.	Checking out/returning library materials	1	2	3	4
b.	Finding books on the shelves	1	2	3	4
c.	Listening and viewing audiovisual materials	1	2	3	4
d.	Obtaining magazines	1	2	3	4
e.	Reference assistance	1	2	3	4
f.	Using LINCC, for books or databases	1	2	3	4

OVER PLEASE ....

Central Florida Community College

5. **Please rate the following statements on a scale of 1 to 3.**

                                 (1=agree, 2=disagree, 3=no opinion)

a.	Circulation staff is helpful and efficient.	1 2 3
b.	Group study rooms are available when I need them.	1 2 3
c.	Library instruction classes are helpful and informative.	1 2 3
d.	Photocopy services in the library serve my needs.	1 2 3
e.	Reference faculty are helpful in finding information.	1 2 3
f.	The library has enough viewing stations for videos and other audiovisual materials.	1 2 3
g.	The library has the materials I need, books, magazines, AV materials, databases, etc.	1 2 3
h.	The library is open when I can use its services.	1 2 3
i.	The library provides access to quiet study spaces.	1 2 3

6. **How would you rate the Library/Learning Resources Department overall?**

                             Excellent   Good   Fair   Poor

7. **What is the most positive statement you can make about the Library/Learning Resources Department and its services?**

_____

_____

_____

8. **What is the most negative statement you can make about the Library/Learning Resources Department and its services?**

_____

_____

_____

9. **Are there any other comments, compliments or constructive suggestions, you would like to add?**

_____

_____

_____

Thank you for helping us better serve you.

Central Florida Community College

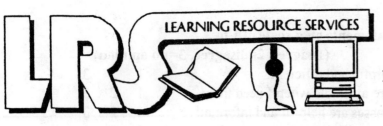

LEARNING RESOURCE SERVICES

Libraries • Media Centers • Computer Centers

STUDENT SURVEY

THE LEARNING RESOURCE SERVICES (LRS) WOULD LIKE TO KNOW MORE ABOUT
HOW YOU USE OUR SERVICES AND WHAT YOU THINK ABOUT SERVICES PROVIDED.

- Please do *NOT* sign your name to this confidential survey form.
- If you have filled out this survey in another class, do not fill it out again. Instead check here and return
  the survey to your instructor. *(NOTE: This is not the same survey you may have seen in the library.)* ❏
- Written comments can be made in the spaces (front and back) provided on the green answer sheet.
- When you have completed the survey return it to your instructor.
  Thank you for your help.

Please use a #2 pencil and mark your answers on the machine readable form.

Section I: Use

I use the following LRS services:

	Library	*Media Center*	*Computer Center*
at instructor's suggestion	1. (a) *yes* (b) *no*	2. (a) *yes* (b) *no*	3. (a) *yes* (b) *no*
as a course requirement	4. (a) *yes* (b) *no*	5. (a) *yes* (b) *no*	6. (a) *yes* (b) *no*
personal learning	7. (a) *yes* (b) *no*	8. (a) *yes* (b) *no*	9. (a) *yes* (b) *no*

For items 10 - 29, please mark all that apply.
I use LRS services at:

Library
10. (a) Cypress Creek   (b) Eastridge   (c) Northridge   (d) Pinnacle   (e) none of these
11. (a) Robbins   (b) Rio Grande   (c) Riverside   (d) Fredericksburg   (e) none of these
12. (a) Reagan   (b) Round Rock   (c) San Marcos   (d) none of these

Media Center
13. (a) Cypress Creek   (b) Eastridge   (c) Northridge   (d) Pinnacle   (e) none of these
14. (a) Robbins   (b) Rio Grande   (c) Riverside   (d) Fredericksburg   (e) none of these
15. (a) Reagan   (b) Round Rock   (c) San Marcos   (d) none of these

Computer Center
16. (a) Cypress Creek   (b) Eastridge   (c) Northridge   (d) Pinnacle   (e) none of these
17. (a) Robbins   (b) Rio Grande   (c) Riverside   (d) Fredericksburg   (e) none of these
18. (a) Reagan   (b) Round Rock   (c) San Marcos   (d) none of these

How often have you used LRS services at these sites?:

	Daily	Weekly	Monthly	Few Times a Semester	Never
19. Cypress Creek	(a)	(b)	(c)	(d)	(e)
20. Eastridge	(a)	(b)	(c)	(d)	(e)
21. Northridge	(a)	(b)	(c)	(d)	(e)
22. Pinnacle	(a)	(b)	(c)	(d)	(e)
23. Robbins	(a)	(b)	(c)	(d)	(e)
24. Rio Grande	(a)	(b)	(c)	(d)	(e)
25. Riverside	(a)	(b)	(c)	(d)	(e)
26. Fredericksburg	(a)	(b)	(c)	(d)	(e)
27. Reagan	(a)	(b)	(c)	(d)	(e)
28. Round Rock	(a)	(b)	(c)	(d)	(e)
29. San Marcos	(a)	(b)	(c)	(d)	(e)

• •

I have used these LRS services to:

Mark your answers with: (a) *Yes* or (b) *No*

Library
30. do research
31. use periodicals
    (magazines/newspapers)
32. find leisure reading
33. copy audiotapes
34. check out/ return a book
35. study own materials
36. use reserve material
37. make photocopies
38. get help from Librarians
39. use print-based reference materials
40. use computerized indexes and reference sources
41. group study

Media Center
42. view an ITV tape
43. record audiotapes
44. complete a class assignment
45. use audiovisual materials
46. use viewing area
47. work with media staff

Computer Center
48. wordprocess/write a paper
49. use specialized instructional software
50. get help from staff
51. produce instructional materials
52. get a class orientation

• •

53. Do you use other area libraries for ACC work?   (Mark all that apply.)
    (a) no
    (b) University of Texas
    (c) St. Edward's University
    (d) Austin Public Library
    (e) other (*Please explain in area 1 on the answer sheet.*)

54. If you use another library, why? (Mark all that apply.)
    (a) To use specialized collections not available at ACC.
    (b) Library is closer/more convenient to where I live.
    (c) Library is open when ACC libraries are closed.
    (d) Material is available that is often checked out at ACC.
    (e) other (*Please explain in area 1 on the answer sheet.*)

⇨ ⇨ ⇨ ⇨ ⇨
Austin Community College

Section II: Evaluation of Materials and Services

Please describe your level of satisfaction with the following areas:

Mark your answers with: (a) *excellent* (b) *good* (c) *fair* (d) *poor* (e) *not applicable*

Library

55. computer catalog
56. book collection
57. magazine/newspaper collection
58. reference collection
59. reserves process
60. document delivery service/intercampus loan
61. computerized indexes and reference sources
62. hours the library is open
63. equipment (copiers, printers) quality
64. equipment accessibility (location)
65. noise level
66. room temperature
67. library staff

Media Center

68. media collection
69. media equipment
70. media viewing area
71. media center staff
72. noise level

Computer Center

73. software collection
74. computer equipment
75. hours the computer center is open
76. computer center staff
77. noise level

• •

I would rate the LRS staff's:

Mark your answers with: (a) *excellent* (b) *good* (c) *fair* (d) *poor* (e) *not applicable*

78. knowledge/expertise
79. knowledge of equipment
80. ability to help me accomplish my tasks
81. ability to answer my questions
82. courtesy

83. helpfulness
84. accessiblity

• •

85. Have you written a paper that required ACC LRS resources?
    (a) *yes* (b) *no*
86. Have you produced a multimedia product that required ACC LRS resources?
    (a) *yes* (b) *no*

Section III: Future Directions

Please rank your priorities for future additions to the LRS:

Mark your answers with: (a) *High priority* (b) *Medium priority* (c) *Low priority* (d) *Okay as it is*

87. more books
88. more magazine/journal subscriptions
89. more newspaper subscriptions
90. more Library staff
91. more Media staff
92. more Computer Center staff
93. more audiovisual materials
94. more computer software
95. internet access
96. more computer equipment

97. more reference materials
98. longer hours of service
99. more study rooms
100. more equipment for students with disabilities
101. more media viewing equipment
102. more computerized indexes and reference sources
103. more multimedia workstations
104. computers for loan
105. newer computers and peripherals

Austin Community College

Have you ever been unable to use LRS resources because:

Mark your answers with: (a) *often* (b) *sometimes* (c) *rarely* (d) *never*

106. not enough library seating
107. no available computer catalog
108. not enough media viewing stations
109. not enough computer workstations
110. no available computerized indexes and reference sources

111. no help within a reasonable length of time
112. material was not on shelf (e.g., checked out, missing, lost, etc.)
113. needed materials not owned by ACC
114. equipment was not working

Section IV: Personal Data

115. Do you have access to a personal computer other than at ACC?

    (a) *at home* (b) *at work* (c) *elsewhere* (d) *no*

116. Is the computer you use most often

    (a) *PC?* (b) *Mac?*

117. If you have a computer, does it have a modem with a baud rate of at least 9600?

    (a) *yes* (b) *no*

118. With your computer are you able to access the Internet?

    (a) *yes* (b) *no*

119. English is my primary language

    (a) *yes* (b) *no*

120. My age range is

    (a) *16-21* (b) *22-30* (c) *31-49* (d) *50+*

121. I am enrolled

    (a) *at ACC only* (b) *ACC and another institution*

122. I have

    (a) *enrolled at ACC as a new student*   (b) *enrolled at ACC for more than one semester*

    (c) *taken courses at ACC from time to time*

123. I am currently enrolled in

    (a) *one course* (b) *two courses* (c) *three courses* (d) *four courses* (e) *five courses*

124. My primary focus of study is

    (a) *art/humanities* (b) *business/computer science* (c) *social sciences* (d) *vocational/technical* (e) *math/science*
        Or

125. (a) *health science* (b) *parallel studies* (c) *personal enrichment* (d) *undecided*

126. Most of my classes are held at:

    (a) *CYP* (b) *ERG* (c) *NRG* (d) *PIN*
        Or

127. (a) *ROB* (b) *RGC* (c) *RVS* (d) *other*

Thanks for taking the time to give us your opinion!

	1	2	3	4	5	6

1. How often do you use the library?
   1=1-2 times weekly, 2=1-2 times monthly, 3=1-2 times per semester, 4=Never

2. If you answered NEVER to question #1, what is your primary reason for not using the library?   1=don't know where things are   2=don't know how to use it
   3=don't need to use it

   For questions 3 - 9, rank aspects of the library, using the following scale
   1=Excellent, 2=Good, 3=Average, 4=Fair, 5=Poor, 6=Don't know

3. Physical facilities

4. Book collection

5. Periodical Collection and databases

6. Audio Visual Collection

7. Library hours

8. Services of librarians

9. Environment conducive to research and study

For questions 10 & 11, rank library usage using the following scale:
   1=Often, 2=Seldom, 3=Never

10. I use the library to complete course assignments.

11. I use the library for personal reasons rather than for course assignments.

COMMENTS AND SUGGESTIONS

LEARNING RESOURCES DEPARTMENT
CLASSROOM FACULTY SURVEY

Learning Resources Department staff are interested in learning about how often and for what purposes you use our services. We also would like to know what you feel we do well and what you wish we did differently. Your response is important to us since it will be used to improve LRC materials, facilities, and services. Thank you for your help. ___PLEASE CIRCLE APPROPRIATE RESPONSES AND RETURN THE SURVEY TO WANDA JOHNSTON BEFORE FEBRUARY 1ST.___

1.   You primarily teach in
_____Business
_____Communications/Fine Arts
_____Health Occupations
_____Humanities
_____Math, Science & Physical Ed
_____Public Service
_____Technical Education

2.   How often do you use Learning Resources Department services?
_____2-5 times per week
_____1-3 times per month
_____less than once a month
_____never

3.   How often do you use the following learning resources services?
(1=often, 2=sometimes, 3=not at all)

a.	Gathering information for your own instruction	1 2 3
b.	Reviewing materials for your student use	1 2 3
c.	Reserving materials for student assignments/review	1 2 3
d.	Browsing magazines, newspapers, recreational reading	1 2 3
e.	Participating in student library instruction	1 2 3
f.	Using audiovisual materials	1 2 3
g.	Using media production for instructional purposes	1 2 3
h.	Scheduling and using audiovisual equipment	1 2 3

4.   Please rate the following statements on a scale of 1 to 3.
(1=agree, 2=disagree, 3=no opinion)

a.	Library materials adequately support my curricular needs.	1 2 3
b.	The Library has a sufficient collection of resources (books, magazines, videos, etc.) to serve the needs of my students.	1 2 3
c.	The Library has sufficient access to electronic databases.	1 2 3
d.	The department has the audiovisual equipment that I need.	1 2 3
e.	I can rely on audiovisual equipment, in good repair, when and where I need it.	1 2 3
f.	Library faculty provide effective library instruction.	1 2 3
g.	Media materials are created if not available commercially.	1 2 3
h.	Procedures for placing materials on reserve are reliable.	1 2 3
i.	I have input in the development of the library's collections.	1 2 3
j.	The library offers appropriate facilities to serve our needs.	1 2 3

OVER PLEASE ....

Central Florida Community College

5.   How would you rate the Learning Resources Department overall?

Excellent   Good   Fair   Poor

6.   What is the <u>most positive statement</u> you can make that describes your feeling about the Learning Resources Department and the services it provides?

_____

_____

_____

7.   What is the <u>most negative statement</u> you can make that describes your feeling
about the Learning Resources Department and the services it provides?

_____

_____

_____

_____

8.   Are there any other comments, compliments or constructive suggestions, that you would like to add? Are there services you wish we would add? Are there services you would like to learn more about? ...

_____

_____

_____

_____

_____

Thank you for helping us better serve you and your students.

Middle States Self-Study

**Library/Learning Center/Academic Computing
Core Analysis Team**

Teaching Faculty Survey

Fall 1997

Your participation in this survey which is being done as part of the College Middle States self-study process will be very much appreciated. Please return to Debra Ahola, Dept. of Humanities & Social Sciences, Elston Hall 311, by **Wednesday, December 10, 1997.**

You are currently:

    1. Full-time _____   2. Adjunct _____.

      3. Total number of years employed by SCCC (full-time and adjunct) _____.

A.   Begley Library

    1.   Do you give library-related assignments to your students? Yes _____ No _____.

    2.   Do you use the Library for your own research/information needs?
        Yes _____ No _____.

    3.   Do you bring your students to the Library for library skills/bibliographic instruction sessions? Yes _____ No _____.

    4.   How well does Begley Library's collection meet the needs of your students for print and electronic resources?   5   4   3   2   1
                    Very well   Neutral   Not Well

    5.   How well does the Library's print and electronic collection meet your own research/information needs?   5   4   3   2   1
                    Very well   Neutral   Not Well

    6.   How well do the Library's reference librarians meet the needs of your students for assistance in using the Library and its resources?
        5   4   3   2   1
        Very well   Neutral   Not Well

    7.   How well do the Library's reference librarians meet your own needs for assistance in using the Library and its resources?
        5   4   3   2   1
        Very well   Neutral   Not Well

2

8.   If you bring your students to the Library for library skills/bibliographic instruction sessions, how well does this instruction meet the needs of your students?

    5   4   3   2   1

   Very well   Neutral   Not Well

9.   Are there areas of the collection you would like to see improved? Please describe briefly.

10.   Are there ways you would like to see reference services developed or improved? Please comment briefly.

11.   Are there ways you would like to have library skills/bibliographic instruction improved? Please comment briefly.

12.   Do you have any other thoughts or comments about Begley Library and its collection and services?

B.   Media Center

 1.   Do you use the Media Center collection, equipment and services in your instruction?   Yes _____ No _____.

 2.   Please check any audiovisual software items from the collection you have used.

     _____videos
     _____slides
     _____compact disks
     _____16 mm films
     _____other_____

 3.   Please check any Media Center equipment you have used.

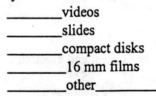

     _____ VCR/TV monitor
     _____ slide projector
     _____ other _____

 4.   Please check any of these Media Center services you have requested.

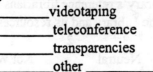

     _____videotaping
     _____teleconference
     _____transparencies
     _____other _____

3

5.   Have you requested videotaping of an instruction-related activity?
     Yes _____ No _____.

6.   Have you attended a teleconference in Begley's TV Studio?
     Yes _____ No _____.

7.   How well does the software collection support your teaching needs?

5	4	3	2	1
Very well		Neutral		Not Well

8.   How well do the equipment resources of the Media Center meet your instructional needs?

5	4	3	2	1
Very well		Neutral		Not Well

9.   How well do the services Media Center staff meet your instructional needs?

5	4	3	2	1
Very well		Neutral		Not Well

10. Are there areas of the software collection you would like to have improved? Please describe briefly.

11. Are there equipment needs that need to be addressed? Please describe briefly.

12. Are there ways you would like to see Media Center services developed or improved? Please comment briefly.

13. Do you have other thoughts or comments about the Media Center and its collection, equipment and services?

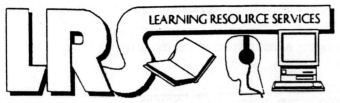

Libraries • Media Centers • Computer Centers

FACULTY SURVEY

THE LEARNING RESOURCE SERVICES (LRS) WOULD LIKE TO KNOW MORE ABOUT
HOW YOU USE OUR SERVICES AND WHAT YOU THINK ABOUT SERVICES PROVIDED.

- Please do *NOT* sign your name to this confidential survey form.
- *(NOTE: This is not the same survey you may have recently filled out in the library.)*
- Written comments can be made on the supplemental answer sheet.
- When you have completed the survey return it to Cary Sowell at Northridge LRS.
  Thank you for your help.

Please use a #2 pencil and mark your answers on the machine readable form.

Section I: Personal Data

1. Your home campus is:
   (a) NRG   (b) RGC   (c) RVS   (d) CYP   (e) ERG
   OR
2. (a) PIN   (b) ROB   (c) FBG   (d) REA   (e) ROR
   OR
3. (a) SMC   (b) WWD   (c) other

• •

4. Your status as a faculty member is:
   (a) Full-time   (b) Part-time

5. Your teaching area is:
   (a) Arts/Humanities   (b) Business/Computer Science   (c) Social Sciences   (d) Vocational/Technical
   OR
6. (a) Math/Sciences   (b) Health Sciences   (c) Parallel Studies   (d) other (*Please respond on the supplemental answer sheet*)

7. When do you most often teach: (Mark all that apply.)
   (a) Morning   (b) Afternoon   (c) Evening   (d) Saturday   (e) Sunday

8. Do you have access to a personal computer other than at ACC?
   (a) yes   (b) no

9. Does your computer have a modem with a baud rate of at least 9600?
   (a) yes   (b) no   (c) Do not have a computer

10. If you have access to a computer are you able to access the internet and/or the World Wide Web?
    (a) yes, through ACC   (b) yes, through another provider   (c) yes, through both *a* and *b*
    (d) no   (e) do not have a computer

11. Are you currently involved in teaching courses through Distance Education?
    (a) yes   (b) no

12. Are you currently involved in using Internet to teach your courses?
    (a) yes   (b) no

- 1 -

⇨ ⇨ ⇨ ⇨ ⇨

Austin Community College

13. Would you be interested in exploring ways the LRS staff could help you and your students access information or complete assignments from home?

(a) yes   (b) no

Section II: Use

How often have you used the following LRS services?

Mark your answers with: (a) *daily*   (b) *weekly*   (c) *monthly*   (d) *few times a semester*   (e) *never*

14. Library at your home campus?

15. LRS/Media Center at your home campus?

16. How often do you use the computer center at your home campus?

17. In courses you teach, how often do you use media programs from the LRC collection (films, compact disk, slides, videocassettes, etc.) in the classroom?

• •

18. In courses you teach, how often do you use audio-visual equipment (16mm/overhead/slide projectors, video players/monitors, video projectors, lecternettes, screens/accessories) from the ACC LRS?

(a) daily   (b) weekly   (c) monthly   (d) once a semester   (e) never

19. If you use the equipment, is it set up on time?

(a) almost always   (b) usually   (c) about half of the time   (d) rarely   (e) do not use equipment

20. Do you use ACC LRS at other campuses also?

(a) yes   (b) no

21. Do you use other area libraries for ACC work? (Mark all that apply.)

(a) no   (b) University of Texas   (c) St. Edward's University

(d) Austin Public Library   (e) other (*Please explain on the supplemental answer sheet.*)

22. If you use other libraries, why? (Mark all that apply.)

(a) They have material ACC lacks.   (b) They have material that is often checked out at ACC.

(c) They are closer/more convenient to where I live.   (d) They are open when ACC libraries are closed.

(e) other. (*Please explain on the supplemental answer sheet.*)

23. Do you believe that using the LRS improves a student's class performance?

(a) yes   (b) no

24. For your students, use of media material (audiotapes, video, etc.) is:

(a) required   (b) encouraged   (c) not mentioned

25. For your students, use of the LRS Computer Center is:

(a) required   (b) encouraged   (c) not mentioned

26. For your students, use of the ACC libraries is:

(a) required   (b) encouraged   (c) not mentioned

27. For your students, use of other area libraries (e.g. UT, St. Edwards, Austin Public, etc.) is:

(a) required   (b) encouraged   (c) not mentioned

28. For your students, library use instruction is:

(a) extremely important   (b) somewhat important   (c) not important

29. Do you currently integrate use of the ACC LRC within your courses?

(a) yes   (b) no

30. What do you believe is the best method to introduce students to the LRC resources and services?

(a) Classroom presentation by LRC staff for a course assignment.   (d) Tour of the LRC without a course assignment.

(b) Paper based orientation for a course assignment.   (e) other (*Please explain on the supplemental answer sheet.*)

(c) Tour of the LRC for a course assignment.

Austin Community College

31. Were you aware that as a faculty member you have an opportunity for input concerning purchase of materials for your academic discipline?

   (a) yes   (b) no

• •

Have you used the Library to:

Mark your answers with: (a) *Yes* or (b) *No*

32. do research?
33. checkout/return books?
34. request books from other libraries through Interlibrary Loan?
35. request books or magazine articles (document delivery) from another ACC campus?

36. request books or magazines for purchase?
37. review print materials in the collection related to your discipline?
38. talk to staff about integrating library assignments into your course?
39. Read books & periodicals for enjoyment?
40. Use indexes to maintain awareness of current publications?

• •

Have you used the LRS Media Center to:

Mark your answers with: (a) *Yes* or (b) *No*

41. checkout/return audiovisual material?
42. checkout/return media equipment?
43. work with media staff to produce instructional materials?
44. request production of materials?

45. request other services (photography, off-air taping, computer support)?
46. request media programs for preview/purchase?
47. review media materials in the collection related to your discipline?
48. talk to staff about integrating media-related assignments into your course?

• •

Have you used the LRS Computer Center to:

Mark your answers with: (a) *Yes* or (b) *No*

49. use specialized instructional software?
50. use faculty productivity area?
51. check your e-mail?
52. produce instructional materials?
53. give a class orientation?

54. request computer software for preview/purchase?
55. review computer software and other computer materials in the collection related to your discipline?
56. talk to staff about integrating computer-based assignments into your course?

• •

Have you used the Instructional Development Specialists to:

Mark your answers with: (a) *Yes* or (b) *No*

57. help you research current trends and uses of technology in your field?
58. help you find software to support your content and course objectives?
59. suggest ways in which to use multimedia presentations, computer software or the computer lab to bring technology into your courses?
60. design and develop or help you develop computer-based material to use in your courses?
61. assist in the preparation of Mini-Grant applications?
62. develop and present training on technology tools for groups of interested faculty?

• •

63. Have you used the electronic indexes (on CD ROM workstations or the on-line catalog) available for locating citations or full-text articles from magazines and newspapers?

   (a) yes   (b) no

64. Are there other electronic resources you would like to see in the library?

   (a) yes   (b) no

   If yes, what resources? (Please respond on the supplemental answer sheet.)

⇨ ⇨ ⇨ ⇨ ⇨

Austin Community College

Section III: Evaluation of Materials and Services

Please rate the following LRS services:

Mark your answers with: (a) *excellent*   (b) *good*   (c) *fair*   (d) *poor*   (e) *never used*

Library
65. Staff availability
66. Staff knowledge/expertise
67. Staff courtesy/helpfulness
68. Book collections
69. Checkout process
70. Reference service
71. Reserves process
72. Periodicals collection
73. Intercampus loan/doc delivery
74. Hours open
75. Space
76. Availability of seating

Media Center
77. Staff availability
78. Staff knowledge/expertise
79. Staff courtesy/helpfulness
80. Media collection
81. Equipment
82. Media viewing area
83. AV production capability
84. Hours open
85. Space
86. Availability of seating

Computer Center
87. Staff availability
88. Staff knowledge/expertise
89. Staff courtesy/helpfulness
90. Software collection
91. Computer equipment
92. Hours open
93. Space

• •

I have repeatedly encountered problems in these areas:

Mark your answers with: (a) *Yes* or (b) *No*

Libraries
94. Needed materials not owned by ACC
95. Items not on shelves (missing/checked-out)
96. Not enough library seating
97. Not enough computerized library catalogs
98. Not enough computerized periodicals/
    reference databases
99. Help in a reasonable amount of time
100. Other (*Please explain on the supplemental
    answer sheet.*)

Media Centers
101. Not enough media viewing stations
102. Need more equipment/classroom use
103. Help in a reasonable amount of time
104. Not enough media programs
105. Other (*Please explain on the
    supplemental answer sheet.*)

Computer Centers
106. Not enough computer
    workstations
107. Computer Center network down
108. Not enough computer software
109. Help in a reasonable amount
    of time
110. Other (*Please explain on the
    supplemental answer sheet.*)

Section IV: Future Directions

Please rate your priorities for future additions to the LRS.

Mark your answers with: (a) *very important*   (b) *somewhat important*   (c) *not important*   (d) *no opinion*

108. more books
109. more periodicals
110. hire more staff
111. more audio visual materials

112. more computer software
113. internet access
114. more computer equipment
115. more media viewing equipment

Thanks for taking the time to give us your opinion!

Comments - Nursing Department Meeting 2/9/98.

B) Using the attached information describing resources in this program area, please provide specific recommendations for the improvement or development of Library/Media resources relevant to Program # 15 .   Be as specific as possible.

1. Library print resources: *Very accommodating.*

2. Accessibility of print resources: *Wonderful - staff will help with search of any kind.*

3. Library electronic resources: *Can access holdings and obtain hard copies.*

4. Accessibility of electronic resources: *Would like to be able to access journal articles from faculty offices*

5. Media resources: *Accommodating - ex Accommodating - some outdated. We've bought what we use in videos, etc.*

6. Accessibility of media resources: *Good.*

7. Availability of media equipment: *Need more multi-media classrooms*

8. Equipment quality, maintenance and repair: *Come promptly for repairs.*

9. Services provided by librarians: *Excellent service in all ways (SAS classes, data, reprints, etc,*

10. Services provided by library and media support staff: *Excellent - ex. Susan Bless doing Internet sessions.*

11. Production services: *Excellent - esp. for nursing students - doing taping for us - very accommodating*

12. Other library services: *Excellent - a lovely facility*

C) Please provide specific recommendations, particularly new resources or initiatives in the following areas:

1. Information resources - books, periodicals, government documents, audiovisual materials, electronic databases:

    We make ongoing requests and will continue to do so.

2. Instructional services - library instruction, reference, circulation, reserve, etc.:

    We will continue to use the reserve section, Fall SAS classes, etc.

3. Media services - equipment - availability (classroom and loan), maintenance and repair; production services - TV studio, taping (audio and video):

    Would like to have "sign out" laptop computers.
    Please continue taping of classes in N221.
    N221 - Computer disappeared that just needed disk - would like that service available.

4. Technology resources - application and use of computer technology - consultant services, equipment access, network/internet use, etc.:

    Would like journal articles on line in offices.

5. Other suggested new innovations in resources or services. Specifically, in what ways can the Library/Media Services help improve the quality of learning and teaching in Program # 15

    Concern with distance learning and library access for these students.
    Media center could apply for grants to develop instructional materials (ie power Point, videos) in conjunction with faculty to be more production oriented.

Emily Wisley at Nursing Department Meeting
Completed By

2/9/98
Date

CENTRAL FLORIDA COMMUNITY COLLEGE
LEARNING RESOURCE CENTER

Reference Satisfaction Survey

PLEASE LET US KNOW HOW WE ARE DOING. Evaluate the *reference* service that you received today by circling one number on each of the following scales. Feel free to explain—use the back of the form.

If you were NOT asking a reference question today, please check here _____ and stop. Thank you.

1. *Relevance* of information provided:

   Not relevant   1   2   3   4   5   Very relevant

2. Satisfaction with the *amount* of information provided:

   Not satisfied   1   2   3   4   5   Very satisfied
   (too little, too much)   (the right amount)

3. *Completeness* of the answer that you received:

   Not complete   1   2   3   4   5   Very complete

4. *Helpfulness* of staff:

   Not helpful   1   2   3   4   5   Extraordinarily helpful

5. Overall, how *satisfied* are you?

   Not satisfied   1   2   3   4   5   Extremely satisfied

   Why? _____

   _____

6. You are:

   _____ 1. Undergraduate   _____ 4. Research staff
   _____ 2. Graduate student   _____ 5. Other staff
   _____ 3. Faculty   _____ 6. Other?_____

7. What will you use this information for?

   _____ 1. Course work   _____ 4. Mix of several purposes
   _____ 2. Research   _____ 5. Current awareness
   _____ 3. Teaching   _____ 6. Other?_____

THANK YOU! Please leave this questionnaire in the box.

USE BACK OF PAGE FOR ANY ADDITIONAL COMMENTS.

Central Florida Community College

TECHNICAL COLLEGE OF THE LOWCOUNTRY
LEARNING RESOURCE CENTER

EVALUATION OF LRC ORIENTATION

Please rate the orientation by choosing one response for each item.

PLEASE USE NO. 2 PENCIL

RIGHT	WRONG

Today's Date

M	M	D	D	Y	Y

Course: _____

Instructor: _____

	Strongly Agree	Agree	Disagree	Strongly Disagree
1. The orientation's purpose was explained prior to the class.	①	②	③	④
2. The librarian appeared knowledgeable.	①	②	③	④
3. The librarian was well prepared.	①	②	③	④
4. The presentation was well organized.	①	②	③	④
5. The amount of material covered was appropriate.	①	②	③	④
6. The length of the orientation was appropriate.	①	②	③	④
7. The overall quality of the session was high.	①	②	③	④

Please use the remaining space for any comments.

Technical College of the Lowcountry

LIBRARY ORIENTATION
NUNEZ COMMUNITY COLLEGE

YES NO

1. Is this your first library orientation at Nunez? _____ _____

2. Are you attending with your class? _____ _____

    If so, what is the course?_____

    Who is your instructor?_____

3. Have you been given a specific task that requires library use? _____ _____

    If so, did the orientation suggest useful resources? _____ _____

4. Did your library instructor ask for your questions? _____ _____

    If so, were they answered adequately? _____ _____

5. Would you feel comfortable asking for help in the future? _____ _____

6. Did the orientation describe/display the following:

    a. Circulation policies and procedures? _____ _____

    b. Use of computerized card catalog? _____ _____

    c. Reference materials? _____ _____

    d. Use of computerized databases? _____ _____

7. Are you more likely to use this library after having the orientation? _____ _____

    Would you have used it anyway? _____ _____

8. Have you previously used libraries to assist in your studies? _____ _____

9. Do you think the library is an inviting place to study and work? _____ _____

    The Nunez College Library staff appreciates your time in completing this form. We hope that this will help us to better serve your library needs. Please write your comments and/or suggestions below.

_____

_____

Elaine P. Nunez Community College

BCC LEARNING RESOURCES CENTER

COMMENTS!!!
QUESTIONS!!!
SUGGESTIONS!!!

_____

_____

_____

_____

_____

_____

_____

_____DATE:_____

SUGGESTED MATERIALS

GENERAL:

SUBJECT _____

SPECIFIC ITEM:

TITLE_____

_____

AUTHOR_____

PLACE IN THE SUGGESTION BOX

APPENDICES

CJCLS Library/Learning Resources Program Review Survey
Contributing Institutions
Bibliography
Federal Register: Focus on Educational Effectiveness
Regional Accrediting Agency Addresses
Regional Accrediting Criteria: Library/Learning Resources
Middle States Association of Colleges and Schools
New England Association of Schools and Colleges: Higher Education
New England Association of Schools and Colleges: Technical and Career
North Central Association of Colleges and Schools
Northwest Association of Schools and Colleges
Southern Association of Colleges and Schools
Western Association of Schools and Colleges
Standards for Community, Junior, and Technical College
Learning Resources Programs
About the Editor and Section

CJCLS LIBRARY/LEARNING RESOURCES PROGRAM REVIEW
SURVEY 1998

Please attach a business card or complete the following:

Name and Title: _____ *85 respondents representing 12% return*
Institution and Address:_____
Phone:_____ FAX:_____
Internet Address:_____

Please place an "x" next to the appropriate response or responses for each question:

1. Number of full-time equivalent (FTE) students, as listed in IPEDS report:
    17%   *15* fewer than 1000 *10%*   *9* 5000-7000
    27%   *23* 1000-3000   *12%*   *10* 7000-10,000
    17%   *15* 3000-5000   *15%*   *13* more than 10,000

2. Number of full-time equivalent staff in your library/learning resources department (include professional, paraprofessional, and clerical, but do not include student assistants):
    22%   *19* fewer than 5   *15%*   *13* 15-25
    33%   *28* 5-10   *6%*   *5* 25-40
    19%   *16* 10-15   *5%*   *4* more than 40

3. For what purposes does your library/learning resources department participate in Library/Learning Resources Program Review?
    Please share a copy of your latest program review report.
    60%   *51* Department Self-Assessment and Planning Purposes
    46%   *39* Institutional Budget/Planning Cycle (*Strategic planning*)
    36%   *31* Annual Report
    66%   *56* As part of Regional Accreditation, e.g. Middle States, SACS, etc.
    22%   *19* State Program Review (*AR,ID,FL,ME,SC,WA,CA,IL,NM,NY,OR,CT*)
    6%   *5* As part of Focused Program Review, please specify:
                Teacher education, NLN, Radiology tech
    4%   *3* Other *System program review, educational master plan*

4. Who participates in the library/learning resources program review?
    84%   *71* Library/Learning Resources Director
    78%   *66* Library/Learning Resources Staff
    28%   *24* Library/Learning Resources Advisory Committee
    54%   *46* College Faculty
    46%   *39* College Students
    42%   *36* College Administration
    51%   *43* Accreditation Self Study Committee
    4%   *3* Other *Division Deans, Library Committee, Community*

--Over please--

5.   What data is included in the library/learning resources program review process?
   86%   _73_ Annual statistical data
   35%   _30_ Longitudinal statistics
   33%   _28_ Comparative statistics with other colleges
   41%   _35_ Comparative statistics with ACRL/AECT Standards
   67%   _57_ User Satisfaction Surveys/Output Measures
   58%   _49_ Goals accomplished during past year
   2%   _2_ Other _Acquisitions, budget, mission/vision, present situation_

6.   If statistical data is compiled, what do you count and how?
   Please share your data gathering instruments and compilation summary.
   89%   _76_ Circulation of resources *(through online system)*
   65%   _55_ Facilities use
   65%   _55_ Reference transactions *(sample weeks)*
   80%   _68_ Library instruction classes *(calendar)*
   48%   _41_ Faculty audiovisual equipment use
   20%   _17_ Media production services
   76%   _65_ Interlibrary loan
   75%   _64_ On site collection size
   21%   _18_ Teleconferences
   8%   _7_ Audiovisual equipment repairs
   11%   _9_ Other *databases, OPAC use, telecourses/enrollments, serials*

7.   If user satisfaction survey/output measures are used, what do you measure and how? *Please share a copy of your survey.*
   a.   Do you survey __3__ faculty, __7__ students, or __53__ both.
   b.   What do you measure?
   62%   _53_ General program satisfaction
   54%   _46_ General program use
   42%   _36_ Library instruction, specifically *classes, students, eval form*
   38%   _32_ Reference service, specifically _____
   25%   _21_ Audiovisual equipment service, specifically *equip quality*
   12%   _10_ Media production, specifically *TV show, video, transparency*
   40%   _34_ Collection holdings and access *general/subject, find needed?*
   24%   _20_ Interlibrary Loan success
   29%   _25_ Suggestion Box input
   5%   _4_ Other *Informal comments, physical facility, computer labs*

CJCLS PLANS TO PUBLISH A COLLECTION OF MODEL LIBRARY/LEARNING RESOURCES PROGRAM REVIEW INSTRUMENTS, PROCEDURES, AND REPORTS. IF YOU ARE WILLING TO SHARE YOURS, PLEASE MAIL THEM BACK WITH THIS SURVEY. WE WILL CONTACT YOU FOR COPYRIGHT RELEASE ON ANY SAMPLES WHICH WILL BE INCLUDED IN THE BOOK.

Please return this survey and documents no later than April 1, 1998, to:

Wanda Johnston
1525 SE 42nd Avenue
Thank you for your assistance with this project!   *Ocala, FL 34471*

CONTRIBUTING INSTITUTIONS

Austin Community College
W. Lee Hisle
Assoc. VP, Learning Resources
1212 Rio Grande Avenue
Austin, TX 78701
(512) 223-3069

Broome Community College
Charles Quagliata
VP for Student & Community Affairs
Box 1017
Binghamton, NY 13902
(607) 778-5199

Bunker Hill Community College
Diane M. Smith
Public Services Librarian
250 New Rutherford Avenue
Boston, MA 02129-2991
(617) 228-2213

Canada College
Marilyn Hayward
Coordinator of Library Services
4200 Farm Hill Blvd.
Redwood City, CA 94061
(650) 306-3476

City College of San Francisco
Rita Jones
Dean of Library/Learning Resources
50 Phelan Avenue, R501
San Francisco, CA 94112
(415) 452-5454

College Center for Library Automation
J. Richard Madaus
Director
1238 Blountstown Highway
Tallahassee, FL 32304
(904) 922-6044

Corning Community College
Barbara Hornick-Lockard
Director of Learning Resources
1 Academic Drive
Corning, NY 14830
(607) 962-9385

De Anza College
James McCarthy
Director of Library Services
21250 Stevens Creek Blvd.
Cupertine, CA 95014
(408) 864-8454

Edmonds Community College
Dale Burke
Technical Services Librarian
20000 68th Avenue West
Lynnwood, WA 98036
(425) 640-1526

Elaine P. Nunez Community College
Karen Leeseberg
Librarian
3710 Paris Road
Chalmette, LA 70043
(504) 278-7440, ext. 244

Florida State Board of Community Colleges
Thomas E. Furlong, Jr.
1314 Turlington Building, DOE
325 West Gaines Street
Tallahassee, FL 32399-0400
(850) 488-1721

Imperial Valley College
Eileen Shackelford
Dean of Learning Services
P.O. Box 158
Imperial, CA 92251
(760) 355-6378

Indian River Community College
Pat Profeta
Head of Library Services
3209 Virginia Avenue
Fort Pierce, FL 34981
(561) 462-4757

Macomb Community College
Kul Gauri
Dean of Academic Services
44575 Garfield Road
Clinton Twp., MI 48033-1139
(810) 286-2014

Montgomery College
Elizabeth Thoms
Librarian
7600 Takoma Avenue
Takoma Park, MD 20912-4197
(301) 650-1493

Northwest Indian College
Nancy Carroll
Library Director
2522 Kwina Road
Bellingham, WA 98226-9217
(360) 676-2772, ext. 214

Pasadena City College
Mary Ann Laun
Director of Library Services
1570 E. Colorado Blvd.
Pasadena, CA 91160-2003
(818) 585-7913

Schenectady Community College
Nancy Heller
Director of Library Services
78 Washington Avenue
Schenectady, NY 12305
(518) 381-1200

Scottsdale Community College
Sharon Howard
Public Services Librarian
9000 East Chaparall Road
Scottsdale, AZ 85250-2699
(602) 423-6654

Southern Ohio College
Jane Myers
Librarian
2791 Mogadore Road
Akron, OH 44312
(330) 733-8766

Spartanburg Technical College
Margaret E. S. Green
Library Director
P.O. Box 4386
Spartanburg, SC 29305
(864) 591-3615

Tarrant County Junior College
Theodore E. Drake
Director of Library Services
1500 Houston Street
Ft. Worth, TX 76119
(817) 515-4513

Technical College of the Lowcountry
Richard Shaw
Director of Learning Resources
921 Ribaut Road, P.O. Box 1288
Beaufort, SC 29902
(843) 525-8304

West Valley College
Dave Fishbaugh
Director of Library Services
14000 Fruitvale Avenue
Saratoga, CA 95070
(408) 741-2140

BIBLIOGRAPHY

Adams, Mignon S., and Jeffrey A. Beck. <u>User Surveys in College Libraries: CLIP Note #23</u>. Chicago: Association of College and Research Libraries, 1995.

  Although focusing on college and small university libraries, this book provides useful examples of user surveys and supporting documents that have been developed by college librarians to obtain feedback from the clientele they serve. Included are general user satisfaction surveys, surveys concerned with one area or aspect of the library, and adaptations of the forms from VanHouse's work. Also included are scripts for focus groups and interviews, sample cover letters, directions and rewards for completed forms, and examples of summary reports.

Altschiller, Donald. "Read Any Good (Suggestion) Books Lately," <u>C&RL News</u> 53(February 1992):92-93.

  Most literature discusses quantitative and qualitative evaluative procedures. This brief article describes the benefits of library suggestion books which encourage library users to write their complaints and comments. In addition, to suggestion books are suggestion boxes in which library users may drop their ideas, comments, and suggestions. Both methods, when coupled with responses, prove a highly effective method for informal information gathering and dissemination.

Baker, Sharon L., and F. Wilfrid Lancaster. <u>The Measurement and Evaluation of Library Services</u>. Arlington, VA: Information Resources Press, 1991.

  This book was designed to help librarians evaluate the effectiveness of library service by familiarizing them with various evaluation techniques. Evaluative techniques are described and evaluated for their rigor and practical application. This work concentrates on collections and materials availability, reference services, and catalog use, as well as the effects of accessibility and ease of use on public services, the range and scope of library services, the relevance of standards to evaluation activities, and evaluation by means of user studies.

Blandy, Susan, Lynne M. Martin, and Mary L. Strife. <u>Assessment and Accountability in Reference Work</u>. New York: Haworth Press, 1992.

  This volume responds to the 1988 publication in the *Federal Register* on educational effectiveness regulations, the nationwide recession affecting library services, and ACRL's *Measuring Academic Library Performance*. Of special note are discussions of general assessment requirements and methodologies and of more specific applications relating to general reference, library instruction, mentoring programs, and facilities. Also included is a case study of a community college's preparation for a Middle States Association accreditation visit.

de Leon Clarke, Tobin. <u>Output Measures Manual for Community College Learning Resource Programs and Libraries</u>. Suisun, CA: Learning Resources Association of California Community Colleges, 1992.

Based on a survey of California library/learning resources administrators, twelve output measures were identified as most valuable for measuring their programs. These include circulation, in-house use, facilities use, reference transactions, library orientation, library skills course completion, faculty audiovisual hardware service, faculty audiovisual software service, media production, user satisfaction, turnover rate, and interlibrary loan fill rate. Each measure includes definitions, directions, and data collection forms.

Evaluation of Reference and Adult Services Committee, Management and Operation of Public Services Section, Reference and Adult Services Division, ALA. <u>The Reference Assessment Manual</u>. Ann Arbor, MI: Pierian Press, 1995.

The Committee's goal is to provide easy access and identification of appropriate evaluation instruments for both public and academic library reference services with the goal that the instruments will be replicated and further improved. Specific topics included are users and questions, materials resources, human resources, the reference process, and results.

Evans, G. Edward. <u>Developing Library and Information Center Collections</u>. Littleton, CO: Libraries Unlimited, 1987.

This work includes a collection evaluation section which addresses questions such as: How useful is the collection? What are the strengths of the collection? How effectively have we spent our collection development moneys? Collection evaluation or assessment projects, using both quantitative and qualitative assessment activities, are described.

Hernon, Peter, and Charles R. McClure. <u>Evaluation and Library Decision Making</u>. Norwood, NJ: Ablex Publishing, 1990.

Evaluation is treated as a research activity essential for appraising the utility of library programs and services and for providing feedback to organizational planning and change. Thus, the purpose of this book is to help the reader in understanding evaluation as a research activity and the relationship between evaluation and planning.

Hernon, Peter, and Ellen Altman. <u>Service Quality in Academic Libraries</u>. Norwood, NJ: Ablex Publishing, 1996.

This book examines service quality, identifies its essential elements (including electronic service delivery), and discusses ways in which service quality can be assessed quantitatively and qualitatively. Based on a two-year research study, this work encourages every library manager to consider the impact of accountability on the library's role within the larger organization and how to narrow the gap between library service and customer expectation.

Lancaster, F.W. If You Want to Evaluate Your Library .... Champaign, IL: University of Illinois, 1993.

This book discusses methods that can be used to evaluate various facets of library service, both the determination of success rate and the identification of reasons for successes and failures. Topics included include document delivery or library collections, reference services, and related evaluation topics, including cost-effectiveness and cost-benefit aspects.

Oberembt, Kenneth J. Annual Reports for College Libraries: CLIP Note #10. Chicago: Association of College and Research Libraries, 1988.

Although prepared for college and small university libraries, this CLIP Note offers ideas for developing or redeveloping the annual report document and encourages its use in strengthening user support for the library. Sample data gathering forms, cover graphics, content graphics, and full annual reports are included.

Sacks, Patricia Ann, and Sara Lou Whildin. Preparing for Accreditation: A Handbook for Academic Librarians. Chicago: American Library Association, 1993.

This practical "how to" handbook was written to assist academic libraries in preparing for external accreditation reviews. The authors approach accreditation as a component of the overall planning, self-study, and assessment processes of an academic institution. Sections include the accrediting environment, accrediting practices and procedures, preparing for the accreditation review, and using accreditation results. Sample documents and worksheets are included.

Shonrock, Diana, ed. Evaluating Library Instruction: Sample Questions, Forms, and Strategies for Practical Use. Chicago: American Library Association, 1996.

To assist library instruction librarians in gathering information about their programs from users, the ALA Library Instruction Round Table Research Committee created this handbook of model questions that could be used to develop surveys and evaluation instruments tailored to individual libraries. The sample questions evaluate instructors, class work, and materials/equipment related to library instruction.

Simas, Robert J. Assessment System for the Evaluation of Learning Resources Programs in Community Colleges. Suisun, CA: Learning Resources Association of California Community Colleges, 1983.

This evaluative instrument was created to facilitate evaluation of a comprehensive learning resources program, either by the local college itself or, more objectively, by a visiting team. Its primary goal is to encourage cooperation between the evaluation team and college personnel to gain better insights into local objectives, capabilities, and needs. Sections on quantitative and qualitative data collection procedures and forms precede a final section describing data analysis and presentation.

Subcommittee on Guidelines for Collection Development, Collection Management and
    Development Committee, Resources and Technical Services Division, ALA.
    Guide to the Evaluation of Library Collections. Chicago: American Library
    Association, 1989.
    This document lists foundation principles of collection evaluation, identifies
various collection evaluation methods, and lists the advantages and disadvantages of each
method currently in use.

VanHouse Nancy A., Beth T. Weil, and Charles R. McClure. Measuring Academic
    Library Performance: A Practical Approach. Chicago: American Library
    Association, 1990.
    This practical manual of measures specific to academic libraries was developed
to present instruments which could measure the impact, efficiency, and effectiveness of
library activities; quantify or explain library output in meaningful ways to administrators;
us used by unit heads to demonstrate performance levels and resource needs; and provide
data useful in library planning. The fifteen measures are grouped into categories of
general satisfaction, materials availability and use, facilities and library uses, and
information services.

FEDERAL REGISTER:
FOCUS ON EDUCATIONAL EFFECTIVENESS

(Federal Register 53:127 July 1, 1988)

602.17 Focus on educational effectiveness.

The Secretary determines whether an accrediting agency, in making its accrediting decisions, systematically obtains and considers substantial and accurate information on the educational effectiveness of post secondary educational institutions or programs, especially as measured by student achievement, by-

a. Determining whether an educational institution or program maintains clearly specified educational objectives consistent with its mission and appropriate in light of the degrees or certificates it awards;

b. Verifying that satisfaction of certificate and degree requirements by all students, including students admitted on the basis of ability to benefit, is reasonably documented, and conforms with commonly accepted standards for the particular certificates and degrees involved, and that institutions or programs confer degrees only on those students who have demonstrated educational achievement as assessed and documented through appropriate measures;

c. Determining that institutions or programs document the educational achievements of their students including students admitted on the basis of ability to benefit, in verifiable and consistent ways, such as evaluation of senior theses, reviews of student portfolios, general educational assessments (e.g., standardized test results, graduate or professional school test results or graduate or professional school placements), job placement rates, licensing examination results, employer evaluations, and other recognized measures;

d. Determining that institutions or programs admitting students on the basis of ability to benefit employ appropriate methods, such as pre-admissions testing or evaluations, for determining that such students are in fact capable of benefiting from the training or education offered;

e. Determining the extent to which institutions or programs broadly and accurately publicize, particularly in representations directed to prospective students, the objectives described in paragraph (a) of this section, the assessment measure described in paragraph (c) of this section, the information obtained through those measures, and the methods described in paragraph (d) of this section, and;

f. Determining the extent to which institutions or programs systematically apply the information obtained through the measures described in paragraph (c) of this section toward steps to foster enhanced student achievement with respect to the degrees or certificates offered by the institution or program.

(Authority: 20 U.S.C. 1058 et al.)
(FR Doc. 88-14912 Filed 6-29-88; 9:14 am)

602.18 Regard for adequate and accurate public disclosure.

The Secretary determines whether an accrediting agency, in making its accrediting decisions, reviews elements of institutional or program integrity as demonstrated by the adequacy and accuracy of disclosures of information that do not mislead the public (and especially prospective students) as to-

a. The institution's or program's resources, admission policies and standards, academic offerings, policies with respect to satisfactory academic progress, fees and other charges, refund policies, and graduation rates and requirements;

b. The institution's or program's educational effectiveness as described in 602.17;

c. Employment of recent alumni related to the education or training offered, in the case of an institution or program offering training to prepare students for gainful employment in a recognized occupation, or where the institution or program makes claims about the rate or type of employment of graduates; and

d. Data supporting any quantitative claims made by the institution with respect to any matters described in paragraphs (a), (b) and (c) of this section.

(Authority: 20 U.S.C. 1058 et al.)
(FR Doc. 88-14912 Filed 6-29-88; 9:14 am)

REGIONAL ACCREDITING AGENCY ADDRESSES

Middle States Association of
  Colleges and Schools
Commission on Higher Education
3624 Market Street
Philadelphia, PA 19104
(215) 662-5605
http://www.msache.org/
DE, DC, MD, NJ, NY, PA, PR, VI

New England Association of
  Schools and Colleges
Commission on Institutions of
  Higher Education
209 Burlington Road
Bedford, MA 01730-1433
(718) 271-0022
http://www.mec.edu/neasc/cihe.htm
CT, ME, MA, NH, RI, VT

New England Association of
  Schools and Colleges
Commission on Technical and
  Career Institutions
209 Burlington Road
Bedford, MA 01730-0950
(718) 271-0022
CT, ME, MA, NH, RI, VT

North Central Association of
  Colleges and Schools
Commission on Institutions of
  Higher Education
30 North LaSalle Street, Suite 2400
Chicago, IL 60602
(312) 263-0456
http://www.ncacihe.org/
AZ, AR, CO, IL, IN, IA, KS, MI,
MN, MO, NE, NM, ND, OH, OK,
SD, WV, WI, WY

Northwest Association of
  Schools and Colleges
Commission on Colleges
11130 NE 33rd Place, Suite 120
Bellevue, WA 98004
(425) 827-2005
AK, ID, MT, NV, OR, UT, WA

Southern Association of
  Colleges and Schools
Commission on Colleges
1866 Southern Lane
Decatur, GA 30033-4097
(404) 679-4500
http://www.sacs.org/
AL, FL, GA, KY, LA, MS, NC,
SC, TN, TX, VA

Western Association of
  Schools and Colleges
Accrediting Commission for
  Community and Junior Colleges
3402 Mendocino Avenue
Santa Rosa, CA 95403
(707) 569-9177
http://wascweb.org.htm/
CA, HI, GUAM, SAMOA

Western Association of
  Schools and Colleges
Accrediting Commission for
  Senior Colleges and Universities
P.O. Box 9990, Mills College
Oakland, CA 94613-0990
(510) 632-5000
http://wascweb.org/senior/
wascsr.htm
CA, HI, GUAM, SAMOA

REGIONAL ACCREDITING CRITERIA:
LIBRARY/LEARNING RESOURCES

MIDDLE STATES ASSOCIATION OF COLLEGES AND SCHOOLS
COMMISSION ON HIGHER EDUCATION

LIBRARY AND LEARNING RESOURCES:
ACCESS AND UTILIZATION

The services, resources, and programs of libraries, broadly defined, are fundamental to the educational mission of an institution and to the teaching and learning process. They support the educational program. They facilitate learning and research activities among students, faculty, and staff.

The scope of library/learning resources, the types of services, and the varieties of print and non-print and electronic media depend on the nature of the institution. They must be in reasonable proportion to the needs to be served, but numbers alone are no assurance of excellence. Of more importance are the quality, accessibility, availability, and delivery of resources on site and elsewhere; their relevance to the institution's current programs; and the degree to which they are actually used. The development of services and collections must relate realistically to the institution's educational mission, goals, curricula, size, complexity, degree level, fiscal support, and its teaching, learning, and research requirements.

An institution should provide access to a broad range of learning resources, at both primary and off-campus sites. Although access to these resources is customarily gained through a library/resource center, an attempt should be made to think beyond the physical confines of the traditional library in regard to information access. A variety of contemporary technologies for accessing learning resources and instruction in their use should be available. In addition to providing broad access to the diffuse world of electronic information, institutions should provide critical reference and specialized program resources at or within easy reach of each instructional location. Where appropriate, institutions should also expand access for users at remote sites, such as extension centers, branch campuses, laboratories, clinical sites, or students' homes.

Each institution should foster optimal use of its learning resources through strategies designed to help students develop information literacy--the ability to locate, evaluate, and use information in order to become independent learners. It should encourage the use of a wide range of non-classroom resources for teaching and learning. It is essential to have an active and continuing program of library orientation and instruction in accessing information, developed collaboratively and supported actively by faculty, librarians, academic deans, and other information providers.

Students, faculty, and staff should have access to remote as well as on-site information resources. An institution can augment its learning resources by drawing upon the special strengths of other institutions and using external services as appropriate. This goal can be achieved through collaboration and resource-sharing or through formal cooperative agreements and networks. Computer and other technological systems can assist in providing convenient access. Interlibrary loan services should be available, well supported, and structured to ensure timely delivery of materials. Multi-campus institutions and those with off-campus programs should design special procedures to provide document delivery as well as sufficient on-site access to learning resources and services.

Teaching faculty, librarians, and other information providers should collaborate on the selection of materials, based on intellectual and cultural depth and breadth. Basic and interpretive books and periodicals and standard reference works should be included. All staff should work together to plan for the management, evaluation, and use of learning resources.

Librarians, information specialists, and other staff must demonstrate their professional competence on the basis of criteria comparable to those for other faculty and staff. They should help facilitate the teaching and learning process, especially in assisting students to improve their information skills. The status of members of the library staff should be commensurate with the significance and responsibilities of their positions.

Library buildings and comparable facilities--whether on or off-campus--should be designed to provide convenient access for users. Such features as seating, lighting, arrangement of books and materials, and acoustical treatment are important and are to be judged by their effectiveness in making the facility an attractive place for study, research, and teaching. Nothing else matters if resources are not used.

Careful evaluation of all learning resources, on-site or elsewhere, should be an ongoing process. A system for assessing the effectiveness of library and learning resources should be available. It should focus on utilization, accessibility, availability, and delivery of materials. Quality and relevance of the collections, effectiveness of reference and referral services, and adequacy of funding for resources and their use are essential. Ultimately, the most important measure will be how effectively students are prepared to become independent, self-directed learners.

Characteristics of Excellence In Higher Education: Standards for Accreditation. Philadelphia: Middle States Association of Colleges and Schools Commission on Higher Education, 1994. pp. 15-16.

NEW ENGLAND ASSOCIATION OF SCHOOLS AND COLLEGES
COMMISSION ON INSTITUTIONS OF HIGHER EDUCATION

STANDARD SEVEN
LIBRARY AND INFORMATION RESOURCES

7.1   The institution makes available the library and information resources necessary for the fulfillment of its mission and purpose.   These resources support the academic and research program and the intellectual and cultural development of students, faculty, and staff.   Library and information resources may include the holdings and necessary services and equipment of libraries, media centers, computer centers, language laboratories, museums, and any other repositories of information required for the support of institutional offerings.   The institution ensures that students use these resources as an integral part of their education.

7.2   Through the institution's ownership or guaranteed access, sufficient collections and services are readily accessible to students wherever programs are located or however they are delivered.   These collections and services are sufficient in equality, level, diversity, quantity, and currency to support and enrich the institution's academic offerings.   The institution provides facilities adequate to house the collections and equipment so as to foster an atmosphere conducive to inquiry, study, and learning among students, faculty, and staff.

7.3   The institution provides sufficient and consistent financial support for the effective maintenance and improvement of the institution's library and information resources.   It makes provision for their proper maintenance and adequate security.   It allocates resources for scholarly support services compatible with its instructional and research programs and the needs of the faculty and students.

7.4   Professionally qualified and numerically adequate staff administer the institution's library and information resources.   The institution provides appropriate orientation and training for use of these resources.   Clear and disseminated policies govern access, usage, and maintenance of library and information resources.

7.5   The institution participates in the exchange of resources and services with other institutions and within networks as necessary to support and supplement its educational programs.

7.6   The institution regularly and systematically evaluates the adequacy and utilization of its library and information resources, and uses the results of the data to improve and increase the effectiveness of these services.

Standards for Accreditation.   Bedford, MA: New England Association of Schools and Colleges Commission on Institutions of Higher Education, 1992.   pp. 23-24.

NEW ENGLAND ASSOCIATION OF SCHOOLS AND COLLEGES
COMMISSION ON TECHNICAL AND CAREER INSTITUTIONS

Standards of Membership
Institutions of Higher Education at the Technical and Career Level

9. LIBRARY AND INFORMATION RESOURCES

The institution provides library resources and services to support its educational programs and the intellectual, cultural, and personal development of its students and staff. The mission and objectives of the Library are consistent with those of the institution. Facility, in partnership with library personnel, demonstrate the importance of information skills and library resources by integrating them into the learning process. Library personnel are involved in curriculum development, resource allocation, and other related activities. Opportunities are provided for faculty and students to participate in the development of library services and collections.

The library staff is sufficient in numbers and professional qualifications to participate actively in the development of educational resources for the institution, while effectively serving users and providing technical support. The institution clearly defines the responsibilities of library personnel, and it provides them with appropriate opportunities for professional development.

Library instruction programs exist to introduce users to the variety of resources and services available. These services are provided for all levels of users. Library services and resources meet users' needs and are well-used. Library hours are adequate and appropriate.

The library provides access to collections that are adequate in quality, level, scope, currency and size to support the institution's mission. This access may be made available through on-site collections and electronic resources, through electronic linkages with other libraries, or through any combination which meets the institution's needs. Selection and deletion of resources are the responsibility of the professional staff, working collaboratively with the college community, and are described in a written policy.

The institution provides an accessible space that is devoted to library use and is adequate in size and comfort for library collections, personnel, and users. Library equipment I up-to-date and properly maintained. Institutions that provide instruction at off-campus locations ensure access to adequate learning resources and services to support the courses and programs offered.

The institution provides sufficient and consistent financial support for the effective maintenance and improvement of the library resources, including collections and equipment.
The institution periodically and systematically evaluates the adequacy and utilization of its learning and information resources and services and makes appropriate changes as necessary.
Revised 3/95

NORTH CENTRAL ASSOCIATION OF COLLEGES AND SCHOOLS
COMMISSION ON INSTITUTIONS OF HIGHER EDUCATION

General Institutional Requirements

18. It provides its students access to those learning resources and support services requisite for its degree programs.

The learning resources referred to in this requirement might differ according to the program. For example, vocational-technical programs cannot succeed without shops and laboratories necessary for effective teaching and learning. Every program requires some use of library resources, broadly defined to include access to information through information networks and computer data bases as well as print media. Similarly, institutions must provide student support services that might include such things as academic advising and financial aid counseling for all institutions, housing and food services for residential colleges, and support programs for targeted constituencies at many colleges. If the institution does not own these resources, it must show that its students have access to them on a regular, dependable basis.

p. 25

Focus on Criterion Two
"The institution has effectively organized the human, financial, and physical resources necessary to accomplish its purposes."

A Special Note on Libraries and Other Learning Resources

Just as writing and critical reading are essential and fundamental academic skills, access to learning resources that contain the world's accumulated and still-developing knowledge is a necessity for students pursuing a higher education. As they have been for centuries, libraries are still the major means by which most students have access to the books, serials, and other materials their studies require. The Commission expects each institution that it accredits to be responsible for assuring that students can and do use the materials essential for their education.

Good practice holds that a basic collection of reserve and course-related readings and reference texts are conveniently available to all of an institution's students (whether on-campus or at other instructional sites). Trained professional librarians (or the equivalent) are essential-to help the institution acquire, store, and retrieve appropriate resources; to assist students in using these resources; and to help students locate and obtain needed resources that the institution does not itself possess.

Institutions should ensure that their off-campus students have access to adequate learning resources. Access of this sort can be provided through the establishment of a branch campus library; by arranging for the site to have regular access to a local librarian, on-line catalog, and book and document delivery services; by making formal arrangements with other appropriate libraries near the site for student use; or by a variety of other means, some only now developing, including placing resources on an institution's Web site or helping students identify some of the selected and dependable Internet sites where appropriate materials are available. Institutions should make **formal** arrangements with other learning resource centers they wish their students to use.

In addition, institutions should continually enhance their collections of books, bound serials, and other print materials with these newer and often more-convenient forms of information storage and retrieval: microforms, CD-ROMs, audiotape. videotape, CDs, on-line databases, connections to the Internet, and others. Making these resources an integral part of a student's education requires the institution to invest seriously in associated hardware and to provide the staff that can maintain these resources, train students in their use, and provide assistance when it is needed.

pp. 37-38

Pattern of Evidence Supporting This Criterion

The institutional self-study process and its subsequent report should review a broad variety of matters. **In developing the pattern of evidence supporting Criterion Two, the Commission suggests the breadth of evaluation that it considers appropriate to it.**

j.   academic resources and equipment (e.g., libraries, electronic services and products, learning resource centers, laboratories and studios, computers) adequate to support the institution's purposes.

p. 39

Focus on Criterion Three
"The instituiton is accomplishing its educational and other purposes."

Assessing the Contribution of Learning Resources to the Education of Students

The requirement that institutions provide their students with access to   books and other requisite learning resources grows out of a broadly-held conviction that the development of critical analytic and research skills requires students to experience a variety of intellectual viewpoints and play an active role in interpreting, evaluating, and synthesizing the information available to them. Therefore, the involvement of the library-and librarians-in the institution's education programs is essential. Faculty and librarians share in the responsibility of emphasizing information literacy in all programs. Implementation of a regularly-updated collection development policy, formulated collaboratively by faculty and library staff, is one hallmark of an institution that takes the educational role of its learning resources seriously; collaboration on course development is another.

Assessing learning resources used by students is yet a third hallmark. Faculty and librarians should move beyond collecting gross circulation numbers to evaluating student use of reference materials and electronic media, and to assessing browsing, circulation transactions (what and to whom), document delivery, and inter-library loans. Higher education library staff need to evaluate their overall efforts, to collect evidence that something worthwhile is happening to students because the library exists. How, where, and in what form to collect this information are up to each institution. and the effective use of the information to improve its learning resources depends on an institution's traditions, structure, orientation, and particular situation.

pp. 47-48

Pattern of Evidence Supporting this Criterion

i.   If appropriate:
        *evidence of support for the stated commitment to basic and applied research through provision of sufficient human, financial. and physical resources to produce effective research

p. 51

Handbook of Accreditation. Second edition. Chicago, IL: North Central Association of Colleges and Schools, 1997.

NORTHWEST ASSOCIATION OF SCHOOLS AND COLLEGES
COMMISSION ON COLLEGES

Standard Five - Library and Information Resources

Standard 5.A - Purpose and Scope

The primary purpose for library and information resources is to support teaching, learning, and if applicable, research in ways consistent with, and supportive of, the institution's mission and goals. Adequate library and information resources and services, at the appropriate level for degrees offered, are available to support the intellectual, cultural, and technical development of students enrolled in courses and programs wherever located and however delivered.

5.A.1 The institution's information resources and services include sufficient holdings, equipment, and personnel in all of its libraries, instructional media and production centers, computer centers, networks, telecommunication facilities, and other repositories of information to accomplish the institution's mission and goals.

5.A.2 The institution's core collection and related information resources are sufficient to support the curriculum.

5.A.3 Information resources and services are determined by the nature of the institution's educational programs and the locations where programs are offered.

Standard 5.B - Information Resources and Services

Information resources and services are sufficient in quality, depth, diversity, and currency to support the institution's curricular offerings.

5.B.1 Equipment and materials are selected, acquired, organized, and maintained to support the educational program.

5.B.2 Library and information resources and services contribute to developing the ability of students, faculty, and staff to use the resources independently and effectively.

5.B.3 Policies, regulations, and procedures for systematic development and management of information resources, in all formats, are documented, updated, and made available to the institution's constituents.

5.B.4 Opportunities are provided for faculty, staff, and students to participate in the planning and development of the library and information resources and services.

5.B.5 Computing and communications services are used to extend the boundaries in obtaining information and data from other sources, including regional, national, and international networks.

Standard 5.C - Facilities and Access

The institution provides adequate facilities for library and information resources, equipment, and personnel. These resources, including collections, are readily available for use by the institution's students, faculty, and staff on the primary campus and where required off-campus.

5.C.1 Library and information resources are readily accessible to all students and faculty. These resources and services are sufficient in quality, level, breadth, quantity, and currency to meet the requirements of the educational program.

5.C.2 In cases of cooperative arrangements with other library and information resources, formal documented agreements are established. These cooperative relationships and externally provided information sources complement rather than substitute for the institution's own adequate and accessible core collection and services.

Standard 5.D - Personnel and Management

Personnel are adequate in number and in area of expertise to provide services in the development and use of library and information resources.

5.D.1 The institution employs a sufficient number of library and information resources staff to provide assistance to users of the library and to students at other learning resources sites.

5.D.2 Library and information resources staff include qualified professional and technical support staff, with required specific competencies, whose responsibilities are clearly defined.

5.D.3 The institution provides opportunities for professional growth for library and information resources professional staff.

5.D.4 Library and information resources and services are organized to support the accomplishment of institutional mission and goals. Organizational arrangements recognize the need for service linkage among complementary resource bases (e.g., libraries, computing facilities, instructional media and telecommunication centers).

5.D.5 The institution consults library and information resources staff in curriculum development.

5.D.6 The institution provides sufficient financial support for library and information resources and services, and for their maintenance and security.

Standard 5.E - Planning and Evaluation

Library and information resources planning activities support teaching and learning functions by facilitating the research and scholarship of students and faculty. Related evaluation processes regularly assess the quality, accessibility, and use of libraries and other information resource repositories and their services to determine the level of effectiveness in support of the educational program.

5.E.1   The institution has a planning process that involves users, library and information resource staff, faculty, and administrators.

5.E.2   The institution, in its planning, recognizes the need for management and technical linkages among information resource bases (e.g., libraries, instructional computing, media production and distribution centers, and telecommunications networks).

5.E.3   The institution regularly and systematically evaluates the quality, adequacy, and utilization of its library and information resources and services, including those provided through cooperative arrangements, and at all locations where courses, programs, or degrees re offered. The institution uses the results of the evaluations to improve the effectiveness of these resources.

Support Documentation for Standard Five

Required Exhibits:

1.   Printed materials that describe for students the hours and services of learning resources facilities such as libraries, computer labs, and audio-visual facilities.

2.   Policies, regulations, and procedures for the development and management of library and information resources, including collection development and weeding.

3.   Statistics on use of library and other learning resources.

4.   Statistics on library collection and inventory of other learning resources.

5.   Assessment measures utilized to determine the adequacy of facilities for the goals of the library and information resources and services.

6.   Assessment measures to determine the adequacy of holdings, information resources and services to support the educational programs both on and off campus.

7.   Data regarding number and assignments of library staff.

8.   Chart showing the organizational arrangements for managing libraries and other information resources (e.g. computing facilities, instructional media, and telecommunication centers).

9.   Comprehensive budget(s) for library and information resources.

10.   Vitae of professional library staff.

11.   Formal, written agreements with other libraries.

12.   Computer usage statistics related to the retrieval of library resources.

13.   Printed information describing user services provided by the computing facility.

14.   Studies or documents describing the evaluation of library and information resources.

Accreditation Handbook. Bellevue, WA: Northwest Association of Schools and Colleges Commission on Colleges, 1996. pp. 68-70.

SOUTHERN ASSOCIATION OF COLLEGES AND SCHOOLS
COMMISSION ON COLLEGES

5.1 Library and Other Learning Resources

5.1.1 Purpose and Scope

Because adequate library and other learning resources and services **are essential** to teaching and learning, each institution **must** ensure that they are available to all faculty members and enrolled students wherever the programs or courses are located and however they are delivered. Each institution **must** develop a purpose statement for its library and other learning resource services. The library and other learning resources **must** be evaluated regularly and systematically to ensure that they are meeting the needs of their users and are supporting the programs and purpose of the institution.

The scope of library and other learning resources, the types of services, and the variety of print and non-print and electronic media depend on the purpose of the institution. Learning resources and services **must** be adequate to support the needs of users. The size of collections and the amount of money spent on resources and services do not ensure adequacy. Of more importance are the quality, relevance, accessibility, availability and delivery of resources and services, and their actual use by students, regardless of location. These considerations **must** be taken into account in evaluating the effectiveness of library and learning resource support. Priorities for acquiring materials and establishing services **must** be determined with the needs of the users in mind.

5.1.2 Services

Each institution **must** ensure that all students and faculty members have access to a broad range of learning resources to support its purpose and programs at both primary and distance learning sites. Basic library services **must** include an orientation program designed to teach new users how to access bibliographic information and other learning resources. Any one of a variety of methods, or a combination of them, may be used for this purpose: formal instruction, lectures, library guides and user aids, self-paced instruction and computer-assisted instruction. Emphasis should be placed on the variety of contemporary technologies used for accessing learning resources. Libraries and learning resource centers **must** provide students with opportunities to learn how to access information in different formats so that they can continue life-long learning. Librarians **must** work cooperatively with faculty members and other information providers in assisting students to use resource materials effectively.

Libraries and learning resource centers should provide point-of-use instruction, personal assistance in conducting library research, and traditional reference services. This should be consistent with the goal of helping students develop information literacy--the ability to locate, evaluate, and use information to become independent life-long learners. Adequate hours **must** be maintained to ensure accessibility to users. Professional assistance should be available at convenient locations during library hours.

Library collections **must** be cataloged and organized in an orderly, easily accessible arrangement following national bibliographical standards and conventions. Students and faculty **must** be provided convenient, effective access to library resources needed in their programs. Convenient, effective access to electronic bibliographic databases, whether on-site or remote, **must** be provided when necessary to support the academic programs.

Libraries and other learning resource centers **must** have adequate physical facilities to house, service and make library collections easily available; modern equipment in good condition for using print and non-print materials; provision for interlibrary loan services designed to ensure timely delivery of materials; and an efficient and appropriate circulation system. Libraries should provide electronic access to materials available within their own system and electronic bibliographic access to materials available elsewhere.

5.1.3 Library Collections

Institutions **must** provide access to essential references and specialized program resources for each instructional location. Access to the library collection **must** be sufficient to support the educational, research and public service programs of the institution. The collections of print and non-print materials **must** be well organized. Institutions offering graduate work **must** provide library resources substantially beyond those required for baccalaureate programs. Librarians, teaching faculty and researchers **must** share in the development of collections, and the institution **must** establish policies defining their involvement.

Each library or learning resource center **must** have a policy governing resource material selection and elimination, and should have a procedure providing for the preservation, replacement or removal of deteriorating materials in the collection.

5.1.4 Information Technology

Although access to learning resources is traditionally gained through a library or learning resource center, a wide variety of contemporary technologies can be used to access learning resource materials. Institutions should supplement their traditional library with access to electronic information. Where appropriate, institutions should use technology to expand access to information for users at remote sites, such as extension centers, branch campuses, laboratories, clinical sites or students' homes. The institution **must** provide evidence that it is incorporating technological advances into its library and other learning resource operations.

5.1.5 Cooperative Agreements

Cooperative agreements with other libraries and agencies should be considered to enhance the resources and services available to an institution's students and faculty members. However, these agreements **must** not be used by institutions to avoid responsibility for providing adequate and readily accessible library resources and services. Cooperative agreements **must** be formalized and regularly evaluated.

5.1.6 Staff

Libraries and other learning resources **must** be adequately staffed by professionals who hold graduate degrees in library science or in related fields such as learning resources of information technology. In exceptional cases, outstanding professional experience and demonstrated competence may substitute for this academic preparation; however, in such cases, the institution **must** justify the exceptions on an individual basis. Because professional or technical training in specialized areas is increasingly important in meeting user needs, professionals with specialized non-library degrees may be employed, where appropriate, to supervise these areas.

The number of library support staff members **must** be adequate. Qualifications or skills needed for these support positions should be defined by the institution.

Organizational relationships, both external and internal to the library, should be clearly specified. Institutional policies concerning faculty status, salary and contractual security for library personnel **must** be clearly defined and made known to all personnel at the time of employment.

5.1.7 Library/ Learning Resources for Distance Learning Activities

For distance learning activities, an institution **must** ensure the provision of and ready access to adequate library/learning resources and services to support the courses, programs and degrees offered. The institution **must** own the library/learning resources, provide access to electronic information available through existing technologies, or provide them through formal agreements. Such agreements should include the use of books and other materials. The institution **must** assign responsibility for providing library/learning resources and services and for ensuring continued access to them at each site.

When formal agreements are established for the provision of library resources and services, they **must** ensure access to library resources pertinent to the programs offered by the institution and include provision for services and resources which support the institution's specific programs--in the field of study and at the degree level offered.

5.2 Instructional Support

To support its curriculum, each institution **must** provide a variety of facilities and instructional support services (e.g., educational equipment and specialized facilities such as laboratories, audiovisual and duplicating services, and learning skills centers) which are organized and administered so as to provide easy access for faculty and student users. They **must** be adequate to allow fulfillment of the institutional purpose and contribute to the effectiveness of learning. These requirements **apply** to all programs wherever located or however delivered.

5.3 Information Technology Resources and Systems

Information technology resources and systems are essential components to higher education. An institution **must** provide evidence that it is incorporating technological advances into its operations.

Information technology resources **must** support the planning function and the educational program component of the institution at appropriate levels. These resources include computer hardware and software, databases, communication networks, and a trained technical and user services staff.

Although the diversity of educational programs and goals will be a major determining factor in the selection of information technology resources by an institution, there **must** be a reasonable infusion of information technology into the curricula so that students exit with the fundamental knowledge and basic ability to use these resources in everyday life and in future occupations. Institutions **must** provide the means by which students may acquire basic competencies in the use of computers and related information technology resources. A reliable data network should be available so that students, faculty and staff may become accustomed to electronic communication and familiar with accessing national and global information resources. There **must** be provisions for ongoing training of faculty and staff members so that they may make skillful use of appropriate application software. These requirements **apply** to all programs wherever located or delivered.

Policies for the allocation and use of information technology resources **must** be clearly stated and consistent with an institution's purpose and goals. These policies **must** be evaluated regularly to ensure that academic and administrative needs are adequately addressed. Appropriate security measures **must** be installed and monitored to protect the confidentiality and integrity of academic systems, administrative systems, and institutional networks. There should be a clearly defined program for maintaining and replacing equipment and software so that they remain consistent with current technology.

Criteria for Accreditation: Commission on Colleges. Decatur, GA: Southern Association of Colleges and Schools, 1995. pp. 56-61.

WESTERN ASSOCIATION OF SCHOOLS AND COLLEGES
ACCREDITING COMMISSION FOR COMMUNITY AND JUNIOR COLLEGES

STANDARD SIX: INFORMATION AND LEARNING RESOURCES

Information and learning resources and services are sufficient in quality, depth, diversity, and currentness to support the institution's intellectual and cultural activities and programs in whatever format and wherever they are offered. The institution provides training so that information and learning resources may be used effectively and efficiently.

1. Information and learning resources, and any equipment needed to access the holdings of libraries, media centers, computer centers, databases and other repositories, are sufficient to support the courses, programs, and degrees wherever offered.

2. Appropriate educational equipment and materials are selected, acquired, organized, and maintained to help fulfill the institution's purposes and support the educational program. Institutional policies and procedures ensure faculty involvement.

3. Information and learning resources are readily accessible to students, faculty, and administrators.

4. The institution has professionally qualified staff to provide appropriate support to users of information and learning resources, including training in the effective application of information technology to student learning.

5. The institution provides sufficient and consistent financial support for the effective maintenance, security, and improvement of its information and learning resources.

6. When the institution relies on other institutions or other sources for information and learning resources to support its educational programs, it documents that formal agreements exist and that such resources and services are adequate, easily accessible, and utilized.

7. The institution plans for and systematically evaluates the adequacy and effectiveness of its learning and information resources and services and makes appropriate changes as necessary.

Handbook Of Accreditation and Policy Manual. Santa Rosa, CA: Western Association of Schools and Colleges Accrediting Commission for Community and Junior Colleges, 1996. pp. 25-26.

Standards for community, junior, and technical college learning resources programs[1]

The final version, approved by ACRL, ALA, and AECT in 1994

These revised standards apply to two-year or three-year academic institutions awarding associate degrees or certificates. They are intended to assist in evaluating and developing learning resources/library programs. With approval by the Association for Educational Communications and Technology and the Association of College and Research Libraries, the document revises and replaces "Standards for Community, Junior, and Technical College Learning Resources Programs," 1990. To remain current and useful, these standards should be reviewed and revised or rewritten on a regular five-year cycle.

Community, junior, and technical colleges make a significant contribution to post-secondary education. Academic programs parallel the first two years of education in the arts and sciences in four-year institutions. Many two-year colleges, and four-year colleges and universities have articulation agreements facilitating student transfers. Reflecting the combination of availability of courses and the expectation of successful completion of programs, more than half of the students currently pursuing higher education are enrolled in community, technical, and junior colleges. The colleges are generally community based and responsive to local needs, offering weekend and evening courses. Many colleges offer contractual courses designed to meet the special training requirements of businesses, corporations, and associations.

Moderate costs and open-access offer opportunities to students who would not otherwise be able to attend college. Emphases on vocational and adult programs and continuing education provide retraining and employment skills for many adult students. Basic education and remediation programs are common offerings.

Comprehensive standards for learning resources programs and services are required to realize the vision of the American Association of Community Colleges of building communities[2] and to maintain excellence in teaching in two-year colleges. In most two-year institutions an expanded concept of learning resources provides diverse instructional services to the broader college community.

The term "learning resources program" is applied in these standards to an organizational configuration which provides a core of library and media materials and a variety of related services. Many programs provide unique or specialized services or have instructional responsibilities. At some colleges, library and learning resources are integrated. At others, they are parallel programs. In some, libraries are separate organizational units. The structure and function of a learning resources program within an institution are determined by the role assigned to learning resources in the institutional organization. This role must be consistent with the stated mission of the institution and its educational goals, curricula, size, and complexity; and include the diverse resources needed to accommodate different learning styles. Generally, these standards apply to a single campus location providing the basic services and activities as listed in appendix A.

The role of the learning resources program is related to the institutional effectiveness of the college. If institutional effectiveness is measured in terms of student success in grades, credit and completion/transfer rates, learning resources standards based on circulation statis-

Prepared by a joint committee of the Association for Educational Communications and Technology (AECT) and ACRL, co-chairs Marilyn McDonald and Gretchen H. Neill

Source: <u>C&RL News</u> 55(October 1994):572-585.

tics, book counts, and other traditional measures may not be relevant because they are limited in detailing the direct impact of learning resources programs in effecting successful learning outcomes. Learning resources effectiveness measures should rely on the relational attributes of the program which directly impact learning attained by students.

Contents

Standard One: Objectives

1.0 The college shall develop a comprehensive mission statement for the learning resources program based on the nature and purpose of the institution.

Commentary. A clear, unambiguous statement of the role of the learning resources program which relates to the effectiveness of the institution is essential for accountability, administration, and review regardless of the organizational structure of the program. For multicollege districts and multicampus community colleges separate mission statements may be needed for each college or each campus which relate to the overall statement for the districtwide learning resources program.

1.1 The mission statement shall be developed by the learning resources staff in consultation with the widest possible representation of the college community and shall be reviewed periodically.

Commentary. Assignment of responsibility to the learning resources staff for the development of the statement and for its utilization and re-

view is appropriate. To be meaningful and useful, the statement needs to incorporate the concerns of the college at large and the relationship of the college to the community.

1.2 The mission statement shall be used, along with institutional educational goals, in the annual planning process.

Commentary. The mission statement serves as a basis for the evaluation of services and the projection of future needs. As such, it becomes an integral part of the planning process and the starting point for institutional effectiveness review of the learning resources programs.

1.3 All component units of the learning resources program, whether administered centrally or by campus units, should be clearly defined.

Commentary. The learning resources program should include essential learning resources and media services as identified in the lists in Appendix A. Centralized and campus-based services should be clearly identified. The learning resources program may include special components beyond learning resources and media services such as those listed in Appendix B.

How these standards were revised

"Standards for Community, Junior, and Technical College Learning Resources Programs" was prepared by a joint committee of the Community College Association for Instructional Technology (CCAIT) of AECT and the Community and Junior College Libraries Section (CJCLS) of ACRL. Members of the committee are Susan M. Anderson, St. Petersburg Junior College (editor); Bernard Fradkin, College of DuPage; Khan M. Hassan (1992–93), Piedmont Virginia Community College; Wanda K. Johnston, Broome Community College; Susan M. Maltese, Oakton Community College; Lois I. Marriott, Southwestern College; Marilyn M. McDonald, Foothill College (co-chair); Gretchen H. Neill, DeKalb College (co-chair); James O. Wallace, San Antonio College (emeritus); Maj. Jerry Klopfer (1993–94), New Mexico Military Institute; and George Wilson, Tyler Junior College.

In establishing the need for joint revision, the members of the committee worked to actively encourage cooperation between ACRL and AECT. The standards were in committee for two years and represent an examination of the professional literature, testimony from a hearing held at AECT in February 1994, a hearing held at the ALA Annual Conference in June 1994, and input from a number of previous users. A draft revision was published in both *Tech Trends* and *C&RL News* (May 1994). ACRL and ALA approved the standards in June 1994 and AECT approved them in August 1994.

1.4 The learning resources program shall be an integral part of the institution's process for the improvement of instruction.

Commentary. An effective learning resources program is an essential component of the entire educational program. Participation by learning resources staff in curriculum development is necessary to plan effective learning resources services, to identify and acquire resources to support the curriculum, and to set priorities on the use of financial and other resources.

Standard Two: Organization and Administration

2.0 The responsibilities and functions of the component units of the learning resources program within the institutional structure shall be clearly defined.

Commentary. The administration of the institution should clearly assign responsibility for the learning resources program and identify the component units. The organizational chart should reflect the services provided and relate to the quality of the overall educational program. When restricted to only core services, the quality and impact on the instructional program may be limited; when too vaguely defined valuable resources may be too widely dispersed to be fully utilized. Clarity in identifying functions and specificity in assigning responsibilities provide a learning resources program capable of supporting the instructional needs of the students and the college community. The learning resources program should develop policies, procedures, and job descriptions and relate these to institutional policies and procedures.

2.1 The duties and responsibilities of the chief administrator of the learning resources program shall be clearly defined within the institutional structure.

Commentary. The program administrator is responsible for providing leadership and direction so that the mission of the program is fulfilled. The administrator should report to the chief academic officer and have the same administrative rank and status as other administrators with similar responsibilities. A title such as Dean or Director of Libraries, Instructional Services, or of Learning Resources is appropriate.

2.2 The learning resources program administrator shall be professionally trained and knowledgeable about learning resources, information, and/or media materials and services.

Commentary. The training and experience of the program administrator shall be as a librarian, a media specialist, or an information specialist, with cross-training desirable. The minimal professional degree and prerequisite for the position is a master's degree in library or information science, educational technology or media, or learning resources services. To interact with other administrators and the learning resources staff, the administrator should demonstrate effective management skills. To make decisions on new information services, the administrator should have continuous experience with new and emerging technologies.

2.3 The comprehensive learning resources program shall include a variety of services which are organized into functional units.

Commentary. The type of component units needed and included will vary from institution to institution and campus to campus. Some possibilities are: access services, public services, telecommunication/Internet connections, technical services, media services, learning development, reprographic services, professional materials services, video production, graphics production, learning laboratories, and computer services. A listing of many of these can be found in the appendices. Services which are not administratively under the learning resources program should be in a coordinating relationship to allow comprehensive planning and reporting and to avoid duplication. For example, if a different program has responsibility for instructional computing, the learning resources program should cooperate in an advisory and consulting capacity since various computer resources are major components of the contemporary learning resource center.

2.4 The administrator and professional staff should be involved in all areas and at all levels of academic activities and institutional planning.

Commentary. Professional staff members should be involved in major college committees and participate in faculty governance to the same extent as other faculty. The program administrator should meet regularly with other college administrators and department heads and, along with professional staff members, be involved in planning, implementing, and evaluating the instructional program of the college.

2.5 Advisory committees should be formed to provide essential information to the staff and to serve as a link with users.

Commentary. To ensure that the learning resources program is responsive to its users and to develop and evaluate effective services, advisory committees should be appointed, elected, or selected by the appropriate faculty, staff, or student constituencies.

2.6 Administration of the learning resources program should be based on staff participation and consensus.

Commentary. While the program administrator is ultimately responsible for the program, participatory governance through regular staff meetings and internal communication should be encouraged. The administrator is responsible for reporting to the staff on institutional policies, procedures, plans, budgets, personnel, and curriculum; in turn the administrator represents the learning resources staff to the college administration.

Each professional and support staff member should be provided with a position description which clearly identifies the duties and responsibilities of the position and superior and subordinate relationships. Performance appraisal standards must be clearly defined and understood by all staff members. A general learning resources manual which provides policy and procedural statements, staff respon-sibilities and duties, items of general information, and learning resources governance and operational statements shall be made available to all staff members.

Standard Three: Staff

3.0 Sufficient and qualified professional and support staff should be available to implement the services for which the program is responsible.

Commentary. Table A evaluates the requirements for adequate numbers of staff on a single campus. The figures are for full-time positions at two levels, minimum and excellent, based on full-time equivalent student enrollments. The table does not include services listed in Appendix B as peripheral. If any of these extra services are assigned, additional positions will be needed. There is a direct relationship between staff, budget, and services. When staff level and funding level increase, the number of services possible will also increase; the reverse is also true. Another factor which affects staff requirements is the ratio of total enrollment to full-time equivalent students. Headcount enrollment is often 50% greater than student full-time equivalent (FTE). The higher the ratio the greater will be the need for additional staff beyond the formulas in Table A. If there is a regular summer session at the college, the positions in Table A should be based on an eleven or twelve month equivalency. If,

Table A*
Staffing Requirements for Single-Campus Services**

FTE Students	Administrators	Professional		Technicians		Other Staff***		Total Staff	
	Min & Excel	Min	Excel	Min	Excel	Min	Excel	Min	Excel
under 1,000	1	2	4	2	4	2	3	7	12
1,000–2,999	1	3	5	3	6	3	6	10	18
3,000–4,999	1	5	7	5	8	4	8	15	24
5,000–6,999	1	7	9	7	12	6	11	21	33
7,000–8,999	1	8	11	9	17	7	14	25	43
9,000–10,999	1	10	15	11	20	9	17	31	53
11,000–12,999	2	14	21	13	24	11	20	40	67
13,000–14,999	2	16	24	16	28	13	24	47	78
15,000–16,999	2	18	27	19	32	16	28	55	89
17,000–19,000	2	20	30	21	36	18	32	61	100

*Does not include student assistants
**Additional staff will be needed if enrollment is 50% greater than FTE
***Secretaries, clerks, lab aides, etc.

in a multicampus or multicollege district, some services are centralized, for example, technical services and automation, personnel will be needed at a centralized site in addition to those needed in the campus libraries.

3.1 The professional staff members shall have a graduate degree from an accredited institution and shall have faculty status, benefits, and obligations or the equivalent.

Commentary. The complexity of the learning resources program may require considerable differentiated staffing by individuals with widely varied professional education and areas of specialization. All should have the same status, benefits, and recognition as other faculty and where faculty rank exists they should meet the same requirements for promotion and tenure as other faculty.

3.2 Professional staff should belong to and participate in library, learning resources, media, and other appropriate associations. Professional development should be encouraged through direct financial support of attendance and participation in local, state, and national organizations.

Commentary. The mark of a professional is not only performance on the job but also knowledge of trends within the profession and technological developments learned from conferences, workshops, and journals; and by assuming leadership within the field.

3.3 The changing nature of learning resources programs and ongoing changes in technology mandate regular staff participation in continuing education.

Commentary. Duty schedules should be flexible enough for staff to pursue job-related training and education, in-service workshops, and conferences and meetings during working hours. The institutional budget should include provision for travel and fees, and release time for in-service training, and education.

3.4 Technical and classified personnel should have appropriate specialized training or experience. Classification, status, and salary should be equivalent to those provided for other institutional employees with similar qualifications.

Commentary. Requirements for training and experience needed should relate to the duties assigned. The relative importance of each type of skill will vary across organizational levels. Supervisors should be selected on the basis of knowledge, experience, and human relations skills.

3.5 Student assistants perform a variety of tasks that assist and complement professional staff, clerical staff, and technicians. Student assistant programs offer work opportunities and career exploration for student workers.

Commentary. The tasks performed by student assistants are usually routine, although some students bring advanced or technical skills which supplement the skills of the regular staff. Permanent staff should supervise and instruct student workers.

Standard Four: Budget

4.0 The mission statement should form the basis for the program budget and be part of the institutional planning process; annual objectives should be developed by the learning resources staff.

Commentary. The mission statement and annual objectives form the basis for the program budget. Stable and consistent funding for acquisitions based on an approved collection development policy is necessary for effective service. Inconsistent funding is the most detrimental element in the development of learning resources collections.

4.1 An ample and stable budget should be based either on a percentage of educational and general budget totals for the institution as shown in Table B or based on a dollar amount per full-time student equivalent as shown in Table C.

Commentary. Basing the learning resources budget totals on a percentage of the college educational or general fund is the preferred approach, but many variables make it difficult to determine the dollar amount of a

Table B*

Learning Resources Budget As % of Educational & General Expenditures

Size	Minimum	Excellent
All	6%	9%

*Appendix B activities and services will require additional funding

percentage during the budget planning process. Capital funds are not included in the percentage except for acquisition of learning resources materials.

A formula using a dollar figure per full-time student equivalent provides a more stable basis for planning collections and services than using a percentage. Table C is based on 1992 dollars; inflation requires these figures to be adjusted upward accordingly. There is a correlation between services, collection, and staff size and the level of expenditures.

4.2 Local processes should be developed so that all expenditures originate within the learning resources program and are reviewed by the chief administrator.

Commentary. Management involves responsibility for expenditures and approval of payments. Budgeting cost analyses and financial planning depend on adequate records. To take advantage of discounts, purchases of materials should be exempt from restrictive bidding and should permit online ordering and standing orders.

4.3 Internal accounts should be maintained for evaluating the flow of expenditures, monitoring encumbrances, and approving payment of invoices.

Commentary. An accurate account of expenditures in categories that are meaningful to the institution is necessary for fiscal accountability, for monitoring status of accounts, for decision making, and for planning.

4.4 The learning resources budget should provide stable funding for contractual services, equipment and materials replacement, and for maintenance of automated public and technical services.

Commentary. Many services are based on continuing support. They cannot be interrupted without serious constraint on the ability to perform effectively. The materials in the collection will become stagnant without a three to five percent replacement of older materials each year.

Table C[3]
Dollar Expenditure by Percentile Per FTE Student for Learning Resources by Category

Category	Minimum 50%ile	Excellent 90%ile
	$	$
Salaries & Wages	92.97	177.74
Print Materials	14.69	37.47
Current Serials	8.70	22.20
Microforms	2.11	6.91
Machine Readable	1.25	6.24
Audiovisual Material	3.12	10.04
Other Material	1.43	6.33
Preservation	0.34	2.07
Equipment	5.41	24.00
Contract Computer	3.21	11.08
Telecommunications	0.67	3.39
Computer Hardware	4.27	15.30
All Other Expenditure	10.30	38.99
Postage	0.29	1.27

4.5 All directly related revenues such as fines, payments for lost and damaged materials, sale of unneeded items, and student use fees, should be used solely for the support of collections, services, and activities of learning resources programs.

Standard Five: User Services

5.0 The learning resources program should provide a variety of services that support and expand the instructional capabilities of the institution.

Commentary. Learning resources programs exist to facilitate and improve education by supporting and expanding classroom instruction and to provide the instructional function of teaching students information-seeking skills for self-directed studies and lifelong learning. As an integral part of the total educational program of the institution, the learning resources program provides instructional as well as support services to students, faculty, and staff which can be demonstrated by the ratio of users to enrollment.

The primary purpose of the learning resources program is to promote learning related to the curriculum of the institution. To do this the learning resources program should provide the best possible access to information in print, media, or electronic format, and have the means for delivering the information to individual users, groups, and classrooms. Access should be from the institution's own collection of materials paired with efficient supportive equipment and services. To integrate new information and new instructional technologies into the curriculum, access and delivery systems should be extended through such means as cooperative borrowing (ILL), resource sharing, renting or leasing services and materials, and the use of electronic databases and other technologies as listed in the appendices.

Students should have access to materials and professional assistance at all times the facility is open. Faculty members should have access to basic instructional media production assistance and assistance in research projects.

5.1 The learning resources program should seek to enlarge access to the academic services available at the college and in the community in accordance with the college mission through networking, resource sharing, online information services, and technological advances.

Table D
Longevity and/or Obsolescence of Information Access Equipment

Equipment Type	Years
16mm projector	10
Slide projector	11
Sound slide projector	8
Sound filmstrip projector	9
Overhead projector	11
Opaque projector	14
Audiocassette recorder	9
Record player	9
Portable PA system	7
Videocassette recorder	7
Television monitor/receiver	9
Video camera/camcorder	5
Microcomputer system	5
LCD panel	4
Video projector	5
CD-ROM player	5
Microform reader/printer	6
Telefacsimile equipment	3

Rapid changes in technology affect equipment life spans as obsolescence becomes as great a factor as longevity.

Source: Wanda K. Johnston, *Administering the Community College Learning Resources Program* (Boston: G.K. Hall Ref., 1994), p. 93. *Reprinted with permission.*

Commentary. Institutional self-sufficiency is no longer desirable or feasible; and provision must be made to utilize new delivery systems. New technologies and new services should be adopted as they become useful to meet institutional goals. The administrator should be prepared to bring to the attention of the faculty and administration new information formats and services as they emerge.

5.2 Services provided should meet the instructional and informational needs of students, faculty, staff, and administration; should provide professional assistance; and should include a minimum of information access provision for students in off-campus locations.

Commentary. Professional staff must be accessible to students to help them gain the skills needed to become self-reliant and critical users of information services. Close cooperation with classroom instructional faculty is mandatory. Off-campus services must be supported by the institution or by contracted services through another library in accordance with ACRL's "Guidelines for Extended Campus Library Services."

5.3 Necessary equipment to access information and to assist instruction should be available and efficiently managed.

Commentary. Equipment must be available when and where it is needed. Equipment may be kept permanently in appropriate classrooms or where materials are found. Equipment must be maintained in good operating condition and should be replaced on a scheduled basis, taking into consideration obsolescence and operating condition (see Table D). Capital funds must be available to insure that advantage can be taken of technological advances. The test for this standard is that less than 10% of the available instructional equipment is inoperable at any time.

5.4 Provision should be made for instructional support production services.

Commentary. Minimum production services should consist of

visualization services, such as overhead transparencies and projected visuals; and audio services, such as recording of lectures and speeches; and duplication of these. As staff and budget allow additional production capabilities should be added to meet instructional requirements.

5.5 An information literacy program for students should be provided through a variety of techniques.

Commentary. A major responsibility of the learning resources program is to provide instruction in locating, accessing, and evaluating information resources in a variety of formats or locations. In addition to general orientation programs, bibliographic instruction may use many different methods, including group and individual instruction and credit or noncredit courses. Basic reference service should provide individualized assistance at all hours the facility is open. The goal is to prepare students for lifetime use of information resources.

Standard Six: Collections

6.0 The learning resources program shall make available an organized collection of materials and information in diversified formats including print and nonprint media, computer software, optical storage technologies, and other.

Commentary. The institution should be prepared to utilize new technologies for accessing information as they are developed. All types of materials conveying intellectual content, artistic and literary works, programmed texts, and packaged instruction are considered resources for effective teaching and learning along with books, periodicals, newspapers, government documents, and microforms. Media materials, including those locally produced, play a vital role in the instructional program of most two-year colleges. The increasing volume of specialized, high-quality information recorded on videotape at relatively low cost gives the videocassette format a key role in delivering current information across all disciplines. Computer software must be treated as a curricular resource. Online computer services and Internet access are increasingly important as information resources along with CD-ROM and video disc technologies.

Table E provides collection goals using definitions from the *Integrated Postsecondary Education Data System* (IPEDS) of the U.S. Department of Education. Quantities under the various columns can be interchanged according to the mission of the institution. For example, an institution with a very strong music program may need to develop a collection of sound recordings or video recordings in excess of these quantitative standards but may need less of some other items. The basis for evaluation in such a case would be the total holdings for that size institution.

6.1 A collection development policy statement shall serve as the basis for selection and acquisition of materials.

Commentary. Acquiring materials based on a written policy with clear guidelines for selection is the nature of collection development. The statement should be developed in consultation with instructional faculty, students, and administrators. Although there are many alternative ways of writing a collection development policy, the following essentials should be included:

a. The purpose for which resources are required.

b. The primary clientele who are to be served.

c. The kinds of materials which are to be acquired.

d. The various factors of cost and suitability which will be considered in determining acquisition priorities.

e. The procedures for handing new types of materials, such as computer software and videocassettes, in conformance to copyright law.

f. The process for leasing or renting materials not readily available or too expensive to purchase.

g. Any arrangements with other institutions for resource sharing, cooperative collections, production, or distribution activities.

h. A statement in support of intellectual freedom and the "Library Bill of Rights."

i. A policy on the acceptance and incorporation of gifts into the holdings which recognizes inherent processing and storage costs.

j. A policy for the de-selection or withdrawal of materials and a method to discard or dispose of them.

6.2 The selection of materials should be coordinated by the professional staff, working closely with the campus community. Final management decisions as to the order in which materials are to be purchased and what gifts should be accepted and processed are the responsibility of the program administrator.

Commentary. Professionally trained librarians and information specialists, because of their knowledge of the collection, are best able to give systematic attention to collection development. Knowledge of existing holdings, identified weaknesses, and acquisitions decisions requires the systematic attention of professional librarians. They should have access to bibliographical tools and reviewing sources for effective collection development.

6.3 The collection shall be of sufficient scope and currency to support the curriculum as well as meet individual information needs of students and faculty.

Commentary. The mission of the college will determine the complexity of the collection, but an institutional commitment to excellence means building and maintaining collections that adequately support: liberal arts and sciences programs to prepare students fully for transfer to four-year colleges and universities; programs that have specialized accreditation (fields such as allied health); vocational and technical programs; special programs for job training, retraining, or upgrading of skills through continuing and community education services; and needed remedial programs for nontraditional or underprepared learners. A broad spectrum of materials must be available to meet research assignments, classroom reports, and self-paced learning.

Table E

Size of Collection for a Single Campus

Minimum Collection

FTE Students	Volumes	Current Serials Subs.	Video & Film	Other Items*	Total Collection
under 1,000	30,000	230	140	2,500	32,870
1,000–2,999	40,000	300	400	5,100	45,800
3,000–4,999	60,000	500	750	8,000	69,250
5,000–6,999	80,000	700	1,250	10,000	91,950
7,000–8,999	95,000	850	1,600	12,000	109,450
9,000–10,999	110,000	900	1,800	14,800	127,500
11,000–12,999	125,000	1,000	2,000	17,400	145,400
13,000–14,999	140,000	1,200	2,200	19,800	163,200
15,000–16,999	155,000	1,500	2,400	22,000	180,900
17,000–19,000	170,000	1,800	2,600	24,000	198,400

Excellent Collection

FTE Students	Volumes	Current Serials Subs.	Video & Film	Other Items*	Total Collection
under 1,000	45,000	400	560	5,000	50,960
1,000–2,999	60,000	600	800	8,000	69,400
3,000–4,999	85,000	800	1,300	11,600	98,700
5,000–6,999	112,000	1,000	2,250	18,000	133,250
7,000–8,999	136,000	1,200	3,000	21,000	161,200
9,000–10,999	166,000	1,400	3,300	26,000	196,700
11,000–12,999	200,000	1,600	4,000	31,000	236,600
13,000–14,999	240,000	1,800	4,500	35,000	281,300
15,000–16,999	285,000	2,100	5,000	41,000	333,100
17,000–19,000	320,000	2,400	5,600	50,000	378,000

*Includes microforms, cartographic, graphic, audio, and machine-readable materials.

6.4 Obsolete, worn-out, and inappropriate materials should be removed based on a policy statement.

Commentary. De-selection or withdrawal on a regular basis is indispensable to a useful collection and should be done systematically. A written policy should govern what should be removed, what should be replaced, and what should be permanently retained. Not only do obsolete and inappropriate materials occupy expensive storage space but they also detract from other materials containing important information. From three to five percent of the collection should be replaced annually. The physical condition of the collection should be reviewed regularly and needed repairs to materials should be made.

6.5 The reference collection shall include a wide selection of standard works, with subject bibliographies and periodical indexes in print and electronic formats.

Commentary. Reference is the core of every library or learning resources program and the beginning point for research. The reference collection should be of sufficient breadth and depth to serve the research and informational needs of the campus community.

6.6 Collections should be organized to provide users with full, efficient, and direct access.

Commentary. The choice of a classification system, the type of catalog, and the arrangement of materials are important decisions. Nationally approved systems (such as the Library of Congress [LC] or Dewey classification schemes) and formats (such as Machine Readable Cataloging [MARC]) are standard. Uniform and multiple access through a public access catalog is essential to make available information in all types of formats. The public access catalog should include bibliographic records and information for all formats included in the collection.

Standard Seven: Facilities

7.0 The learning resources program should provide adequate space for housing collections in a variety of formats, for study and research, for public service activities, for staff workrooms and offices, and for basic production.

The total number of assignable square feet recommended for a building that houses these functions can be calculated by applying a formula that reflects:

- number of FTE students enrolled;
- public services provided;
- size and type of collections;
- number of staff members and their needs.

Since some public higher education regulatory agencies issue space formulas for campus facilities, building planners should investigate guidelines that exist in their state early in the planning process. An example of a state-mandated formula is found in Appendix C.

Commentary. Local conditions and unique needs of colleges will determine the ultimate size of the building. Flexibility is desirable in assigning learning resources space. Most services should be housed in a central location on a campus. When components are located elsewhere, this should be based on the most efficient and effective access to services. Facilities must be planned for long-term service, including anticipated growth and changing formats of collections, projected increase of the student population, sufficient space for work areas, equipment, storage, and the needs of users. Space planning must take into account the changing information environment, the need for computer workstations, for transmission and retrieval of information by telecommunication, for media production, and for physical requirements within the building for electrical and telecommunications connections and for services for the physically disabled. Additional space should be provided when special services are included in the learning resources program.

7.1 Student seating should approximate a minimum of 10% of the FTE enrollment. The space for user activities should accommodate a wide variety of learning styles and study situations, should be attractive, comfortable, and designed to encourage use. Different types of seating arrangements should be offered, including:

- individual carrels, 25 sq ft per student;
- tables for four, 25 sq ft per student;
- lounge chairs, 30 sq ft per student;
- computers and workstations, 40 sq ft per student;
- microform reader stations, 35 sq ft per student;
- small group study rooms, 25 sq ft per student.

In addition to seating, public services areas should include space for public access catalogs, current periodicals, indexes, reference and technology delivery areas, display and exhibit space, group bibliographic instruction, group viewing, and study areas for faculty.

Commentary. Proper arrangement and sufficient space for utilization of instructional equipment and materials, for the needs of the physically disabled, and for both quiet individual study and conference and group study is essential. Advances in technology require flexibility and planning for use of specialized equipment, electrical and computer connections, cables, conduits, lighting, environmental control, fire protection, security, and other factors that affect service. The use of telecommunications necessitates computer connections to faculty offices, classrooms, and outside locations.

7.2 The generally accepted formula for books and other bound collections is calculated at 10 bound volumes per assignable square foot. This number should be doubled to 20 volumes per square foot if compact shelving is used. Other materials such as audiovisual, software, microforms, maps, archives, etc. should be converted to volume equivalents by using one of the existing conversion tables available in the literature and should be included in the total stack estimate. Anticipated growth of the collection should be factored into the calculation.

Commentary. By eliminating unnecessary aisles between each range, compact shelving saves space by doubling shelving capacity and should be considered as a method to maximize storage of print materials in areas of the collection not heavily used. Because the system is very heavy, compact shelving will not be suitable unless the floor loading permits.

7.3 Staff space for workrooms, offices, equipment areas, etc. should be in compliance with state and institutional guidelines (7.0). A minimum of 175 square feet per staff member to accommodate new technologies, equipment, and hardware is desirable. Individual offices for professional staff and administrators should be figured at 200 square feet per person (Boss, p. 108).

7.4 New construction and remodeling projects must be in compliance with the Americans with Disabilities Act (ADA) enacted July 1990.

7.5 Space assigned to learning resources should be restricted to the functions for which it was designed.

Commentary. Space designed for learning resources use should not be used for other institutional activities.

Notes

1. The term "learning resources program" refers to an umbrella organization which encompasses a variety of services. Other frequently used titles for this program include: library services, educational support services, and instructional services.

2. See American Association of Community and Junior Colleges, *Building Communities: A Vision for the New Century, A Report of the Commission on the Future of Community Colleges*, 1988.

3. *Statistical Norms for College and University Libraries: Derived from U. S. Department of Education Fall 1992 Survey of College and University Libraries* (Boulder, Colo.: John Minter Assoc., 1993).

References

"ACRL guidelines for extended campus library services." *C&RL News* 51 (April 1990): 353.

American Association of Community and Junior Colleges. *Building Communities: A Vision for the New Century, A Report of the Commission on the Future of Community Colleges.* 1988.

Boss, Richard. *Information Technologies and Space Planning for Libraries and Information Centers.* Boston: G.K. Hall Ref., 1987.

Johnston, Wanda K. *Administering the Community College Learning Resources Program.* Boston: G.K Hall Ref., 1994.

Martin, Ron G. *Libraries for the Future: Planning Buildings That Work.* Papers from the LAMA Buildings Pre-Conference, June 27–28, 1991. Chicago: ALA, 1992.

Merril, Irving, and Harold Drob. *Criteria for Planning the College and University Learning Resources Center.* Washington, D.C.: AECT, 1977.

Metcalf, Keyes, et al. *Planning Academic and Research Library Buildings, second edition.* Chicago: ALA, 1986.

APPENDIX A: CHECKLIST OF BASIC LRC SERVICES AND ACTIVITIES

Listed below are specific services which are considered to be normal and basic library services in two-year college learning resources or emerging program budgets. This list may not include future or emerging technologies and services. Inclusion does not mean that an institution should have every activity or service listed.

Acquisitions, cataloging, maintenance, preservation, and/or circulation of:
- Audiovisual materials/programs
- Books
- College archives including institutional publications
- Computer programs
- Government documents
- Laser optical (CD-ROM) resources
- Local history materials
- Microforms
- Periodicals
- Special collections

Computer systems management and maintenance:
- Computer programs
- Gateway and Internet access
- Integrated automation systems
- Local area networks (LANs) and wide area networks (WANs)
- Public access computers

Equipment services:
- Equipment inventory, scheduling, and distribution
- Equipment maintenance and repair
- Equipment specifications and purchase
- Group viewing services
- Public access listening/viewing area

Instructional services:

- Bibliographic instruction
- Bibliographies
- Computer literacy
- Copyright consultation
- Group orientation
- Individualized instruction and/or self-paced learning assistance
- Instructional design and development
- Media orientation and instruction
- Online databases searching
- Point-of-use guides, pathfinders, and study guides
- Reference service
- Reserve materials
- Staff development
- Telephone reference

Production services:
- Audio duplication, editing, and recording
- Copy machines, paper and microform
- Drymounting and lamination
- Graphic layout and design
- Interactive video
- Multimedia
- Photography and darkroom
- Satellite communications downlink
- Scripting
- Teleconference services
- Telecourse and distant learning distribution
- Transparencies and slides
- Video duplication, recording, and editing

Resource sharing services:
- Bibliographic networks
- Gateway services
- Interlibrary loan (ILL)
- Internet
- Reciprocal borrowing
- Rental and free-loan materials
- Union catalogs of local resources

"Standards for community, junior, and technical college learning resources programs." *College & Research Libraries News* 51 (September 1990): 757.

Statistical Norms for College & University Libraries: Derived from U.S. Department of Education IPEDS 1992 Survey of Academic Libraries. Boulder, Colo.: John Minter Assoc., 1993.

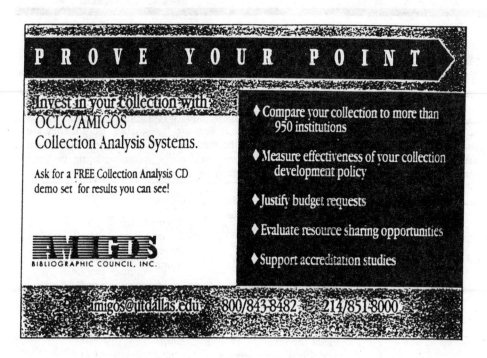
APPENDIX B: CHECKLIST OF ADDITIONAL SERVICES COMPONENTS

This list includes services which require capital funds, space, personnel, and operating budgets in excess of those included in Tables A, B, and C.

Community Services

Curriculum:
- Library technician education
- Bibliographic instruction courses

Faculty Development

Government Documents Depository

Joint-Use:
- Museum
- Other academic library
- Public library
- School library

Laboratories:
- Career
- Learning development
- Literacy
- Self-paced learning
- Testing
- Tutoring

Literacy Programs

Printing:
- College catalogs
- Copy services (not self-serve)
- Literary or other academic college publications
- Print shop

Student ID Service

Television/Radio:
- Radio broadcast
- Satellite uplink
- Telecourse administration
- Telecourse production
- Television broadcast
- Television station/Radio station administration

APPENDIX C

Example: California Community Colleges Facilities Standards—Library Space
(from *Title 5, California Code of Regulations, Section 57030*)

All library space shall be computed by assignable square feet for library functions as specified in the subdivisions of this section. Square feet are "assignable" only if they are usable for the function described. Areas such as the main lobby (excluding card catalogue area), elevators, stairs, walled corridors, restrooms, and areas accommodating building maintenance services are not deemed usable for any of the described functions.

Stack Space	=	.1 ASF x Number of Bound Volumes
		Number of Volumes:
		Initial Increment = 16,000 volumes
		Additional Increments:
		(a) Under 3,000 DGE* = +8 volumes per DGS**
		(b) 3,000-9,000 DGE = +7 volumes per DGS
		(c) Above 9,000 DGE = +6 volumes per DGS

Staff Space	=	140 ASF x Number of FTE Staff) + 400 ASF
		Number of FTE Staff:
		Initial Increment = 3.0 FTE
		Additional Increments:
		(a) Under 3,000 DGE = +.0020 FTE Staff per DGS
		(b) 3,000-9,000 DGE = +.0015 FTE Staff per DGS
		(c) Above 9,000 DGE = +.0010 FTE Staff per DGS

Reader Station Space	=	27.5 ASF x Number of Reader Stations
		Number of Reader Stations:
		Initial Increment = 50 stations
		Additional Increments:
		(a) Under 3,000 DGE = +.10 Stations per DGS
		(b) 3,000-9,000 DGE = +.09 Stations per DGS
		(c) Above 9,000 DGE = +.08 Stations per DGS

Total Space	=	Initial Increment = 3,795 ASF
		Additional Increments:
		(a) Under 3,000 DGE = +3.83 ASF per DGS
		(b) 3,000-9,000 DGE = +3.39 ASF per DGS
		(c) Above 9,000 DGE = +2.94 ASF per DGS

For audiovisual and programmed instruction activities associated with library functions, additional areas sized for individual needs but not exceeding the following totals for the district as a whole.

Total Space	=	Initial Increment = 3,500 ASF
		Additional Increments:
		(a) Under 3,000 DGE = 1.50 ASF per DGS
		(b) 3,000-9,000 DGE = 0.75 ASF per DGS
		(c) Above 9,000 DGE = 0.25 ASF per DGS

*Day-Graded Enrollment = use FTES
**Day-Graded Student = use FTES

ABOUT THE EDITOR AND SECTION

Wanda K. Johnston (MALS, Rosary College), former Director of Learning Resources at Central Florida Community College, is a private consultant providing grant writing, general management, program assessment and planning, human resources. and staff teambuilding assistance. She has nearly twenty years experience in community college library/learning resources services, with additional experience in university. college, and public school libraries. She is Past Chair of ACRL/CJCLS and has chaired or served on numerous Association of College and Research Libraries, Association of Educational Communications and Technology, and other committees. She has written a variety of articles on information technology, library instruction, needs assessment and program development, and grant writing. In addition, she co-edited <u>A Copyright Sampler</u> and authored <u>Administering the Community College Learning Resources Program.</u>

The Community and Junior College Libraries Section, an active section of the Association of College and Research Libraries (ALA), has as its mission to contribute to library service and librarianship through activities that relate to libraries and learning resources centers that support the educational programs in community and junior colleges and equivalent institutions. This goal is implemented by more than a dozen standing and ad hoc committees reflecting the interests and activities of section members. The section supports awards, conference programs, and publishing ventures such as this volume.